Montpellier

MONTPELLIER

Photographs by Bob ter Schiphorst
Text by Kurt Brenner

With a Preface by Geneviève Bon

HVA

English translation by Philip Mattson

ISBN 3-89426-008-4

© 1990 by Heidelberger Verlagsanstalt und Druckerei GmbH, Heidelberg

Designed by Daniel Boissière

Typeset and printed by HVA Grafische Betriebe, Heidelberg

Lithos: Fotolito Longo, Frangart

Binding: Klambt-Druck, Speyer

Flamingos in the Pérols Lagoon.
In the background the city
with the blue wall of the Cevennes

Preface

*F*og, pine forests, and lakes charm me. I love the cold. The North and East fascinate me. So when I fell in love with Montpellier, I knew that it was with a city that "wasn't my type." The way Odette de Crécy wasn't Swann's type. And he caught on quickly: the most violent passions are the irreversible ones, the ones with nothing to hold on to or to be compared with.

In spite of a strong maternal legacy – nine centuries of roots in the Hérault – I didn't come to live here until 1964. What did I find? The arts in Montpellier consisted of "Bonjour Monsieur Courbet." Otherwise? Bonsoir! The students weren't at all like Rabelais or Robert Merle's charming Pierre de Siorac: dispersed in anonymous suburban anti-ghettos, one hardly knew more about them than their numbers, which were impressive, but abstract. Local colour? An accent that many were at pains to disguise, and another, in '62, warm and winning, but gone with the winds of the sea. As to legends, I hardly see more than the Rocher de Substantion; and it only opens up over its treasures once a year. Was it boring here? Louis XIV preferred looking over towards Spain, at any rate.

Sure, the years passed. Sure, the city grew, prospered, grew more beautiful, objectively, as my fondness for it did in me. We had a zoo, a Zenith, a Corum, marble, views, ballets, operas, prestige, fame. But this list, like the incompetent and negative evocation preceding it, tends to show that every city can be torn apart or dragged through the mud, and that it would be crazy to love it just for reasonable reasons.

And then came 1890.

Just when I really mean to start talking about love, I notice the coincidence of dates: we have a centennial to celebrate if there ever was one!

In 1890 André Gide came to Montpellier to visit Paul Valéry. He was 21, the latter 19. Gide, who would later recall of his conversations with Valéry, "I find everything turned topsy-turvy in my head," read some passages from the life work he had just begun writing. The poet, in remembrance, dedicated 'The Friendly Wood' ("Le bois amical") to him. But that's not all: the young men take a walk in the Botanical Gardens, where they stay "seated on an old tomb, talking about immortal things."

Then everything changes. The old streets, slumbering "in a dense absence," the plane trees of the Boulevard Henri IV, which were only green, the Peyrou, which was only classical, the architecture of Antigone, which was only beautiful: this tangle of squares, streets, houses, palais, lanes, quays – everything suddenly starts to radiate, transsubstantiate, unveil its soul. Gide and Valéry didn't do all that much down here, but I am their age, and they had their genius, besides! One day they will be my masters. At the time, they are a glossary making my city intelligible to me. One doesn't just love, one begins to understand: that sonorous and balmy evening in the sweetness of June; that blue and yellow and even tender night, with the terraces all achatter; and the violet dawn, when the first cafés open after the ball; and the mornings full of birds and miracles, when everything, even the oldest faces, even the dust and the noise laud its light and transparency. And finally, there are also fountains: "no fame will ever be a match for you, youth of our hearts!" wrote the author of the "Nourritures" . . .

Perhaps that is what this book can make us see. Bob ter Schiphorst and Kurt Brenner are true Montpellierans: the way the customs inspector was a true painter, and the other Rousseau, Jean-Jacques, was a true musician, the divine Marquise a true writer: not by chance, by birth, by atavism; but by passion, by talent, and by the growth of experience. It is no doubt this "elective affinity" to which they owe their magnificent 'clairvoyance.'

Geneviève Bon

Montpellier

The "Lantern" of the Hôtel St. Côme towers over the roofscape of the city's historic centre

Stretching out into the plain of the lower Languedoc, nestling between the bluish foothills of the Cevennes and the shimmering lagoons, lies the city, open to the four winds, glittering under the vibrant light of the South. Like an unflinching guard, the massive form of Pic St. Loup, Montpellier's local mountain, towers to the North over the barren, austere beauty of the Garrigue landscape. For the trader, conqueror, and pirate ships plying the Mediterranean in days of yore, it was a navigational aid and landmark of the old port towns of Melgueil and Maguelone, long before the now thousand-year-old Montpellier was founded on barren, rocky terrain at the crossroads of old North-South and East-West routes.

Approaching the city from the sea, the first thing one notices are the brightly gleaming neo-classical façades of the recently-built satellite city "Antigone," extending in a stately semi-circle reminiscent of antiquity all the way down to the bank of the Lez. Opposite it is the glass-and-concrete skyscraper built at the same time, which serves as the seat of the regional government and whose gleaming bluish façade reflects the city's silhouette, a testimony in itself of its thousand years of dynamic development. Out of the agreeable disarray of rusty-red roofs in the historic centre, whose distinctive shape – akin to a heraldic shield – makes it easy to spot on the city map, a few prominent buildings stand out as points of orientation, while at the same time pointing to the various architectural periods and their historical context.

Take, for example, the neo-Gothic tower of the Church of St. Anne pointing like an arrow towards heaven, or the church nearby dedicated to the city's patron Saint Roch, or the huge sandstone dome of the mid-18th-century Hôtel St. Côme of the architect Jean-Antoine Giral, or, finally, the square, massive twin towers of the Cathedral of St. Peter, the oldest and most hallowed church in Montpellier.

The historic centre evolved in centuries of gradual growth. In contrast, the functionally modern skyscrapers and office buildings of the business and administrative centres called "Polygone" and "Triangle", built in the sixties, like the pale dwelling silos of the satellite city "La Paillade" in the background, bear witness to the more recent hectic growth of the city – and the dimensions involved. To the North, beautiful country homes, harmoniously grouped in gardens with cypresses, cedars, palms, and gnarled centuries-old olive trees, vanish in the hilly landscape as it gradually ascends to the bluish wall of the Cevennes.

The market in the satellite city of La Paillade

Over this ampitheatre resplendent with colour, the eternal sun of the Midi hangs like a chandelier. An azure sky stretches out over this landscape which is open towards the South. There, on the city's periphery, where old vineyards are scattered in parks of pines, but where in recent decades noisy supermarkets and shopping malls teeming with people have multiplied with a hectic rhythm, the growth of the city is almost imperceptibly encroaching on the lagoon's alluvial area. From the other side, the glittering blue of the Mediterranean Sea smiles on the scene.

If the city, then, in this openess seems inviting to the visitor, and the way it sprawls between the Garrigue-covered foothills and the flat, treeless lagoon is not without a unique attractiveness, it nevertheless lacks the spectacular attributes prized by landscape painting. "Although the city is on a hill, there aren't any very picturesque views of it from any side, whereas from individual points inside or at various ends splendid views can be enjoyed," wrote the Austrian travel author Moritz Hartmann in the mid-19th century in his Languedoc diary. There is no silvery, glittering river with elegant bridges to catch the eye, just a rather modest little river at the city's western edge called the Lez, providing a connection to the sea and the fishermen's town of Palavas-les-Flots. There is no wooded mountain range to arrest the eye; rather the sections of town going back to its medieval period are grouped on and around a slight, chalky rise in the terrain near the sea. At its highest point, where the Palace of Justice stands today, the lords of Montpellier, the Guilhem dynasty, once had one of their castles.

Just the same, this city spreading out into the sun-drenched plain of lower Languedoc, with its helter-skelter of ochre-red tiled roofs, has an irrestible, mysterious charm. The visitor falls victim to its spell once he is inside its walls, be it for the peaceful intimacy of its little squares, its appealing rusticity, its bracingly varied climate, or the youthful mobility of its way of life.

The Montpellier painter, poet, and humanist François Dezeuze (1871–1949), whom his fellow citizens called "L'Escoutaire," put his fascination in the following verses (in dialect):

> *O moun nis! O ma vila! O moun poulit Clapàs!*
> *quand te vese dins l'avuglanta sourelhada,*
> *d'un amour d'enfantou moun am es enmascada*
> *e devène jalous das éuses de moun mas . . .*

> *O my nest! O my town! O my pretty pile of rocks!*
> *When I look at you in the blinding sunlight,*
> *my soul is charmed with child-like love,*
> *and I envy the oaks in my yard . . .*

But back to the living present, let us step right into the lively, noisy everyday bustle of the famous old city, let's look around in the squares and streets which once served Alcofribas Rabelais, then a student at the Medical School, as the scene of his pranks. Once one has got as far as the heart of the historic centre, one easily loses one's way in the truly bewildering tangle of winding lanes and streets. Often the dark mass of the houses, turned grey over the centuries, is pushed so closely together that rays of sunlight rarely reach the ground. Looking up, one sees a small gap of the radiantly blue Mediterranean sky and is charmed by the artless play of the sun's rays, the thousand-fold reflections on cracked stone blocks, on window openings and wrought-iron balcony railings.

Place Saint-Roch

A person who has been in the city during the hot months or indeed during the *malaïgue* in July and August, when the drying out of the lagoons spreads a putrid, musty smell over the area, will praise the builders who put the houses so close together that even during these days, their dwellers can move about in their shadows or go about their business in a leisurely manner. There is another advantage to this manner of building: it provides protection from the winds which impetuously sweep through the city now and then, sometimes accompanied by drops in temperature of up to twenty degrees Fahrenheit. The natives distinguish between thirteen of them; some of their names are a weather forecast in themselves, such as *Tramontana, Martin Grec, Narbonnes,* or *Labech.*

Walking through the cozy closeness of the historic centre, the visitor will soon experience one thing which will be repeated in other situations: Montpellier is a discreet beauty, who artfully conceals some of her charms and wealth, thus creating an atmosphere of mystery about herself. With their massive wooden portals, the monumental and often seemingly aloof stone façades that one finds in the labyrinth of little streets give no hint at first glance of the architectural individuality behind them, or of the charm, the quiet, stately interior court-

Place des Martyrs-de-la-Résistance

11

yards, and the southern gardens inviting one to tarry or even to meditate. One only has to take heart and push open one of these countless portals to find oneself in one of the interior spaces of a splendid *hôtel particulier* which the *noblesse de robe,* the royal administrative officials and the members of high financial circles, had built for themselves. They are for the most part in the classical architecture of the 17th and 18th centuries, the Golden Age of Montpellier's architectural history, during which architects such as Charles-Augustin Daviler, Jean-Antoine Giral, Jean Giral, and Antoine Armand were influential in the city's architectural development. Incorporating elements of the Italian Renaissance, but also of traditional Catalonian architecture – Montpellier was, after all a part of the Kingdom of Mallorca until the 17th century – and influenced by Northern-French Gothic, they developed a style of their own which came to be characteristic of Montpellier.

Often these luxurious city *palais* were built over cellar vaults going back to the Middle Ages; their wonderful cross vaults with bosses chiselled from the warm sandstone of Castries, Sussargues, and Beaulieu can be admired today in the Hôtel de Varenne, now the Salle Pétrarque, or in the Hôtel de Patri. The wealth of ideas of these architects is amazing: they gave each of their buildings an unmistakable individual stamp. The largest of the town *palais* is the Hôtel des Trésoriers de la Bourse on the little street of the same name; until the Revolution it was the seat of the provincial financial administration. After entering through the great portal, one is immediately captivated by the harmonious symmetry and the stately character of the court of honour with its sumptuous stairway open on the courtyard side, and with the graceful sculpture of Cupid over the entrance to the second courtyard, which contains a spacious garden. For a while time seems to stand still in the self-restraint of classical proportions. Since the Heidelberg House was established here in 1966 as a meeting place of German and French culture, this *palais,* which always had its place in Montpellier's history, has played its part in spreading international understanding and the European ideal.

Only a few steps away, and not far from the noisy bustle of the Castellane market hall, is the nobly intimate Hôtel de Montcalm. Once more, one is impressed by the art of the mason who fashioned the winding stairway open on the courtyard side.

If some cities of the late Middle Ages preferred sumptuous balconies or combinations of pillars in front of the façades as a characteristic architectural detail, a beautiful stairway open on the courtyard side is characteristic of Montpellier. The sumptuousness and individuality of its workmanship is an indicator of the *palais'* significance. The best examples of this architecture pervading the historic centre, which so impressively document the Mediterranean way of life, veritable gems of the art of the blacksmith and stonemason in their gracefulness, include not only the Hôtel des Trésoriers de France, also called Lunaret or Jacques Cœur, but also Hôtel Mirman (7, place du Marché aux Fleurs), the Hôtel de Manse (4, rue Embouque d'Or), and the Hôtel de Cambacères-Murles (3, rue Sainte Croix).

*"The city lies at the viewer's feet, glistening in
the vibrant light of the Midi . . ."*

13

Fountains on the Esplanade, built in 1724

Once one has somehow extricated oneself from the homey confusion of the narrow streets, one either finds oneself on one of the busy, noisy boulevards forming a large ring around the old centre or is surprised to discover one of the many little squares inviting one to stop or one of the large parks. The squares of Montpellier – what stories couldn't they tell of the thousand-year history of the city, of all the doings of its natives and what became of them!

This first look around inevitably leads the wanderer out of the shady thicket of the narrow streets to the majestic arena of the Place de la Comédie flooded in light; it has been the heart of the city for over a hundred years. The 'Egg' ("Œuf"), as many Montpellierans simply and fondly refer to it after its original form, is the connecting link between the business and administrative complexes of Triangle-Polygone built in the sixties, where the town hall has also found a new home, the adjoining neo-classical Antigone project and the historic centre. Since being transformed to a spacious pedestrian zone in 1986, it seems even more like an open picture book in which one can read vivid accounts of the city's activities. No outstanding social or cultural event can pass by without leaving some trace in the good old "Œuf."

As a continuation of the tradition of the wine market, which was important in the region well into the fifties, in the last few years wine and even book fairs have been held in the summer on this square, and they have proved very popular with the natives. And if one wants to have a look at this or that local celebrity, one need only take a seat for a short time in one of the many cafés lining this city forum; he's bound to turn up in no time.

To the East is the Esplanade-Charles-de-Gaulle with its pattern of plane trees and with its two fountains promising relief from the heat. It not only invites the inhabitants of the city's centre to take a refreshing walk, it also leads to the congress, culture, and opera centre "Corum" built in recent years; it appears to be anchored like a gigantic ocean liner at the eastern end of the Esplanade. On the side towards the historic centre are the beautiful 18th-century Municipal Library, with its many bibliophilic treasures stemming for the most part from private collections; the Hôtel-de-Cabrières-Sabatier, built in the style of the Second Empire, which was bequeathed to the city and is now the Municipal Museum and well worth visiting; and the former Jesuit College, which is striking in its classicism and purity of form. This building complex of the 16th century is probably the most imposing in the city; it testifies to the particularly active role of the Counter-Reformation in Montpellier. For some of the older Montpellierans vivid memories of youth are associated with this classically proportioned building complex: until its removal to the "Citadel" in 1950, the boys' lyceum was in this building. For several years the building has been one of the pivotal points of the city's turbulent cultural life: it not only houses parts of the Municipal Library, but also the Museum Fabre and the still new Gutenberg Mediathèque. The larger of its two interior courtyards, the Cour Jacques Cœur, is the scene of the International Dance Festival and the music festival put on by Radio France and Montpellier. A chapter of more recent cultural history

„La Comédie du livre",
Montpellier's book fair in the spring

Witnesses of times past . . .

was also written in the tasteful restoration of the "Art Nouveau" cinema, "Pathé," whose façade was designed by the architect Loubatié. In the Centre de Rencontre Rabelais, which now belongs to the City, important national and international meetings take place throughout the year. Bubbling fountains before a backdrop of façades of the 17th, 18th, and 19th centuries, people taking a leisurely stroll or businessmen and scientists hurrying to the congress centre, people commenting on the day's events in the sidewalk cafés, and the merry-go-round full of happily yelling children, all make this a place where the vibrant present and the spirit of the past become a homogeneous whole.

Another cozy spot, where the sensitive visitor feels himself in the presence of the *genius loci Montpellierensis,* where he is following the traces of the thousand-year history of the university town and thus that of France itself, is the Place de la Canourgue. Where today the Hôtel Richer-de-Belleval stands – it served as the city's town hall from 1817 to 1971 – was where the Palace of the Lord of Montpellier, Guilhem VI, stood.

Huge hackberry trees, which seem to thrive in Montpellier's climate, provide welcome shade. At the far end of this inviting square, the splendid fountain monument with unicorns clambering over each other, by the sculptor Etienne d'Antoine (1770), is a commanding presence. From this elevated spot, where once stood the Church of the Holy Cross built by Guilhem VI in 1129, one

The cock at the "Pathé" cinema

15

enjoys not only the view of the four massive towers of the Cathedral and the surrounding medieval section of town (the original Medical Faculty), but also one of the Garrigue surrounding the town, of the country homes nestled in stone-pine, cedar, and cypress groves and of the imperturbable giant of the Cevennes greeting from afar, the Pic St. Loup.

Opposite the Hôtel Richer de Belleval is the Hôtel de Cambacérès-Murles. Its classical purity of form is impressive and enhances the integrated, stately character of the square. One can see why Jean Jacques Rousseau, who spent three months in the city in the autumn of 1737, chose this square for his noontime promenades.

A sloping path leads down from this oasis of peace and meditation. In a few minutes one is back in the medieval quarter around the Cathedral of St. Pierre and the former Benedictine monastery of St. Benoît. Close by are the Botanical Gardens. The massive square-hewn-stone facade of the cathedral, its imposing towers, the great stone canopy resting unshakeably on two colossal columns; all bear witness to the importance of Montpellier as a cradle of medical research, as a centre of European intellectual life – and to the role it played in the debate between faith and knowledge. Standing here, the receptive visitor feels the presence of the great men whose names are so intimately bound up with the fame of the University of Montpellier: the presence of Petrarch and Pope Urban V; of Rabelais and Rondelet; of Guy de Chauliac, whose anatomy textbook was the most influential in medieval Europe; of Richer de Bellevall, founder of the Botanical Gardens. At the entrance to the Faculty of Medicine two magnificent bronze statues keep watch over the great tradition of medical research at Montpellier. One statue bears the likeness of François Gigot de Lapeyronie, founder of the Faculty of Surgery and physician to Louis XV; the other the features of Paul-Joseph Barthez, physician to both Louis XVI and Napoleon I. Having passed beneath their rather awe-inspiring bronze gaze, swept along in a crowd of students, one enters the atrium. On a marble plaque one can read the names of those who helped to found this, the oldest extant medical school. The names of these first teachers sound Arabic, Jewish, French, and German; they bear symbolic witness to the intellectual tolerance of the early university. From this room corridors and a beautiful curved staircase lead up to the former episcopal appartments, which serve today as the office of the dean; to the "Salle des Actes", in which doctoral examinations are held; and to the medical library with its rich collection of invaluable manuscripts.

The Unicorn Fountain
by the sculptor Etienne d'Antoine (1770)
on the Place de la Canourgue

Planchon Square, designed by the landscape architect Bühler in 1857. "It is as beautiful as those in Asia Minor . . ." (Valéry Larbaud)

*One of the most spectacular
of Montpellier's many fountains
(Place de la Comédie)*

A Thousand Years of History

How much existed of this city twelve centuries ago, a city which today, with its old buildings, the remains of its fortifications, its low-built old suburbs and modern, functional castles of concrete, spreads far into the plain of the lower Languedoc and is famed for the oldest medical school in Europe? Hardly anything. A "manse," a farmstead lost in the stony Garrigue covered with prickly bushes, which within a few decades would develop into a town. Even today, native Montpellierans fondly refer to their city as "Le Clapas" – a pile of stones.

Montpellier is thus a relatively young city, when compared to those which were already flourishing in the first centuries A.D. in what was later to be called "Septimania": Narbonne, Elne, Béziers, Agde, Lodève, Maguelone, and Nîmes. It was founded on a hill between the coastal plain and the strip of the Garrigue and connected to the sea and the lagoons by the little river called the "Lez." It was situated on or near three transit routes. The first is called the "Cami Roumieu," the 'Way of the Pilgrims,' which crossed the Lez coming from Castelnau, passed through the Faubourg de Nîmes and Rue de la Saunerie of today, and went on towards Pézenas and Béziers. This route took on great importance from the beginning of the 12th century, when the tomb of Saint James (the Greater) was discovered in Compostella, Galicia. The larger and older transit route passed about 2½ miles north of the city's present-day centre, the "Camion Monete," the 'Way of the Mills' (montius, moulares or monnares). This was the old military road of Domitian leading from Beaucaire via Nîmes, Lunel, Ambrussum, Castelnau to Narbonne and Spain. A third important

Statue of Cardinal Hercule de Fleury on the Grand Stairway of the Palace of Justice, built from 1846 to 1853 by Abric at the spot where the palace of the Guilhems once stood

road, which already existed before the 9th century, was "Lou Cami Salinié," the 'Salt Way,' on which the salt was brought from the lagoons. It turned off Domitian's road before Lunel, followed the shores of the lagoons to the south of Mauguio and passed Montpellier to its south and east, continuing on from there into the lagoon landscape of Frontignan.

The Donation of the Count and Countess of Mauguio in 985

The first document to mention Montpellier is dated November 26, 985 and is in the "Liber instrumentorum memorialum" in the Municipal Archives. In it Count Bernard of Melgueil and his wife Senegonde present as a gift to a man named Guilhem a territory consisting of houses, gardens, fields, vineyards, forests, orchards, etc., located in the area of a "monte pestelario." We also learn from this document that this donation was made under Salic law, as the Count, the Countess, and Guilhem were of Frankish origin.

The etymology of the name "Montpellier," which is derived from the definition of the area "in terminium la monte pestelario" in the document of donation, has long been a vexed question. In the opinion of the romance-language scholar, Maurice Grammont, published in 1948 in the *Revue des langues romanes,* the origin of the name has been and will remain a matter of debate. The popular form Monte peslier, Montpeslier, Montpesler was used to arrive at the etymology Mont Peliou, Mons puellarum, 'Hill of Virgins,' Mont de poissons, 'Hill of Fish,' or Mons pistillarius, 'Hill of Spices.' Derivations from Monspessulus, which stems from the Latin pessulus – crossbar *(verrou)* are closer to home: Mons pessulus meant in this explanation the "Mont du Verrou," i. e., the hill "barring" the road. But the etymology could also be derived from Monte petrarium, meaning the "stony hill" – "Le Clapas," in short.

Finally, still another explanation worthy of serious consideration remains; it is based on Monte pestelario, meaning "La montagne du pastel," 'Hill of Pastel,' thus documenting one of the oldest trades in Montpellier, wool dyeing using woad. As indicated above, there is no certain explanation, so may this short description suffice to show the wide variety of etymological theories.

At the Crossroads

Although founded late in a region which had been populated and cultivated for many centuries, Montpellier grew rapidly under the Guilhem dynasty.

How can this surprisingly bold and extremely dynamic urban development out of rural beginnings be explained? What was behind this sudden flourishing of a spot neglected by history for centuries?

Pilgrims, adventurers, occultists, quacks, and scholars stopped at the sanctuary of Notre-Dame-des-Tables, one of the oldest churches of the city, first

The Arch of Triumph, built from 1691 to 1693 by Charles-Augustin Daviler. The medaillons are by Philippe Bertrand

mentioned in 1090. Around the building, the money changers set up their tables *(taulas)*, where they dealt in all the currencies of the French, Italian, and Arabian provinces. In the church the faithful worshipped the statue of a black Virgin which had been brought back from a crusade by Guilhem VI. This original nucleus of the city developed at what is today Jean-Juarès Square, beneath which the remains of the former crypt are still preserved. The municipal authorities have granted public access to this place and built a fine Museum of Local History there. The first Guilhem surrounded the settlement with a wall and fortifications and also built the first castle, which was in the neighbourhood of the Rue de l'Aiguillerie. The rapid and felicitous development is proof of the deft hand and efficiency of the ruling dynasty, as shown in a citizens' charter of August 15, 1204:

"The lord of Montpellier and his predecessors loved the people. They guarded over them and protected them with the power they were endowed with . . . And so the people of Montpellier gladly show their wealth and display it without qualms." The rabbi Benjamin of Tudele, who visited the Jewish congregations of the Mediterranean basin in the 12th century, already recognized Montpellier's cosmopolitan mission: "This is a good spot for commerce, where Christians and Saracens come in crowds to engage in trade, where Arabs from the Gharb, merchants from Lombardy, great Rome, all regions of Egypt, Greece, Gaul, Spain, Genoa, Pisa congregate, speaking all languages." So apparently all preconditions were fulfilled for the metamorphosis of a spot neglected by history for centuries into a centre of busy activity, an international meeting place, and medieval centre of learning – all in the space of a few generations.

Not only the overland routes were favourable to the town's growth. The port of Lattes, just a few miles towards the sea from Montpellier, had profited from the economic flourishing of the area in the eleventh and twelfth centuries and traded with the Orient and the Levant. The wares were loaded on the high sea onto smaller ships, which then brought them up the Lez to the Pont Juvénal. Thus, Montpellier was already exporting great quantities of wine even then, but also olive oil, dyed cloth, leather goods, wool and jewelry. It is obvious that with trade of such proportions the town's banks had to grow accordingly.

Montpellier Under the Rule of the Guilhems
(985–1204)

As has been mentioned, Guilhem I became the first lord of Montpellier and founder of a dynasty that determined the fate of the town for over two hundred years, until the direct line of descent died out at the beginning of the 13th century. The family's history is too complicated to be related in full here, so let the following suffice.

The monumental porch of the Cathedral in the form of a baldachin with two cylindrical pillars (14th century)

The Rue de Condolle – a street with a very special character

The rue Ste. Ursule in the historic centre

Façades on rue Ste. Croix

The neighbourhood of the Cathedral
seen from the Canourgue Terrace

The staircase of the Hôtel de Montcalm
(rue Friperie) with its hollowed-out column

Hôtel St. Côme, the former
Royal College of Surgery

*The Pic St. Loup,
the "Everest of the Garrigue"
(Yves Daunès)*

A miniature replica of the lobby of the
Paris Opera (hôtel Faulquier, rue Boussairolles)

*The neoclassical colonnade
of the railroad station (1847)*

*The rue Condolle
has a flavour of its own*

The Donkey Market (November 2)

34

Flea market on the Mosson (La Paillade)

Market in the satellite city La Paillade

In the beginning, Montpellier was not a single settlement: out towards the Peyrou, it was under the rule of the Guilhem Dynasty, and towards the Esplanade (the "Montpelliéret" of today), it was under the rule and jurisdiction of the bishops of Maguelone. Both parts grew under the massive influx of new townspeople, and soon they grew together. Guilhem V, son of Ermengarde, had the second palace built further to the North, on the Place de la Canourgue, whereas the Bishop of Maguelone had his built in Montpelliéret, at about the spot where today a street reminds us of the Salle-l'Evêque. This Guilhem V led a turbulent and adventurous life. Aged only 16, he began to rebel against the Bishop (1090). Six years later he joined the First Crusade, during which he distinguished himself by particular valour, as witnessed by the "Chanson d'Antioche." In many ways he is a characteristic example of the feudal lord *(seigneur)* of that epoch. As defender of the faith, he embraced a policy of conciliation with the Roman Papacy all his life. After receiving Pope Urban II in 1096, he met Gelasius II, who was recovering from an illness in the castle of the Count of Mauguio in 1118. And his successor, Calixtus II, came twice to Montpellier to see Guilhem V, in 1119 and 1120.

Under Guilhem VII, with the consent of the Bishop of Maguelone, a first joint fortification of the town was planned and built, providing protection for Montpellier and Montpelliéret, a mighty construction 26 ft. high and 1¼ miles long, with 25 towers, 9 town gates, and a moat. This imposing fortification was approximately on the route described today by the boulevards Louis Blanc, Bonne Nouvelle, Sarrail, Victor Hugo, Jeu de Paume, Ledru Rollin, and Henri IV in the historic centre.

The Guilhem Dynasty was at the zenith of its power under Guilhem VIII. But then quarrels over succession, resulting from the turbulent married life of this last Guilhem, led to its decline. King Alphonso of Aragon had sued for the hand of the beautiful Eudoxia, daughter of the Byzantine Emperor. But when her arrival was delayed, he up and married the Princess of Castile, whereupon the jilted Greek Princess fled to Montpellier in disappointment. There Guilhem was so impressed by her beauty that he married her. This marriage produced a daughter, Marie, who will figure prominently in the continuation of the story. However, Guilhem's married life with Eudoxia was not happy. He left her soon afterwards, fell in love with Agnes of Castile at the royal court in Barcelona and married her in 1187. This marriage produced six sons and two daughters, but it was declared illegitimate by Popes Clement III, Celestine III, and Innocence III, so that Eudoxia's daughter Marie was installed as legitimate heir, to the enthusiastic approval of the people of Montpellier, with whom she was very popular. But in spite of the love and loyalty of her subjects, Marie was not spared the cruel whims of fate. After two unhappy marriages, the first having been arranged when she was only twelve, she was married to the handsome Pedro of Aragon with much pomp in the Church of Notre-Dame-des-Tables in 1204, with the populace of Montpellier in enthusiastic attendance. As "dowry," she ceded the rule over Montpellier with the palaces and castles of Lattes, Montferrier, Castries, Frontignan, as well as 15 others, to the Crown of Aragon.

So far, so good. The way the story goes on borders for some on legend. Nevertheless, it must be told, because it is so important for the history of the city. Pedro II was little disposed to fulfilling his marital duties. On the contrary, he was more interested in a beauty in his wife's retinue. The Consuls of the town (today we would perhaps call them aldermen) felt sorry for their lovable but neglected ruler, but they were also worried about the continuation of the ruling dynasty. So they arranged a secret nocturnal tryst for the enamoured Pedro with the object of his desire, but under the cloak of darkness, they slyly brought him his own wife instead! Seeing himself duped, Pedro would have been the last not to appreciate a good practical joke, and from this time on, he displayed loving fondness for his wife. A few days later he returned to Mireval Castle, where Jacques I was conceived, who would later be called "The Conqueror" and become King of Aragon and Lord of Montpellier. All's well that ends well. When the reconciled royal couple returned to Montpellier on horseback, the townspeople received them dancing for joy. Even today, this event is celebrated by the "Dance of the Hobbyhorse."

This Jacques I, King of Aragon, left Montpellier at age 21 to liberate Mallorca from the Saracens, for which deed he was given the name "The Conqueror." Before his death, in 1276, he divided up his territory and invested his second son, Jacques, with the Kingdom of Mallorca and Roussillon. This act set in motion a gradual development which was to have crucial and far-reaching consequences for the Languedoc: gradually the ties of this Mediterranean region to the Kingdom of Mallorca-Aragon became more lax. The French kings Philip the Bold and Philip of Valois left no stones unturned in their efforts to bolster the French crown's centralistic power by extending its influence over this region which provided access to the Mediterranean. In 1349 the last ruler of Mallorca sold his rights to Montpellier to Philip VI of Valois to raise funds for a military undertaking. With that, Montpellier's golden age of independence approached its end. From now on it belonged to the French crown, as did the Languedoc and Provence.

Montpellier and the Consulate

The cosmopolitan character of the town, the predominant tolerance making the peaceful communal life of Jews, Arabs, Genoans, and Spanish a matter of course, was definitely a boon to its development as a mercantile centre, along with its favourable geographic location. A document from the period of the Consulate, dated 1346, states, "The town of Montpellier is the key to the sea of this earth." Although this is of course an exaggeration, it does stress Montpellier's role as an important point for the transferral of commercial goods.

The bold economic development of the 11th and 12th centuries had to have legal and political consequences, as well. The result was a marked emancipation of the townspeople, culminating in the establishment of the Consulate. The feudal lords, for example the Viscount of Béziers, the Count of Toulouse, or the Archbishop of Narbonne, shared their authority with councillors appointed by them and with elected consuls. This sharing of power came about peacefully for the most part, probably as a consequence of the steady growth in influence of the urban elite. To be sure, there was violence in Montpellier when the Consulate was first introduced in 1141, because the townspeople had elected their consuls over the opposition of their feudal lord, Guilhem VI. The latter was even obliged to leave town for a while and barricade himself in his palace in Lattes until, with the support of the Genoans and the Pope, he regained power over the town. So it was not until 1204 that the Consulate was firmly established in Montpellier. However, government by consulate in the Languedoc always bore the stamp of the feudal style of rule from which it had developed. It can in no way be likened to a democratic civic government of today; it is rather the expression of the power structure of urban oligarchies, within which the merchants, for example, had only moderate influence. At that time, the most important figures of the Consulate were for the most part urban patricians, noblemen, and rich burghers, so that the civic governments of the Languedoc of this period are best characterized (to quote E. Le Roy Ladurie) as "aristocratic republics."

The Beginnings of the Medical School

During this period, i. e., the 12th and 13th centuries, Montpellier was a bustling, flourishing town, with its many churches and chapels, the parishes of Notre-Dame-des-Tables, St. Firmin, and St. Denis, with the bishop's seat on the Isle of Maguelone nearby, with the ports of Lattes and Melgueil, and some twenty fortified palaces and castles in the environs. But it had also already become the intellectual centre of the Kingdom of Aragon, where scholars, experts in the healing arts, astrologers, and philosophers from all countries converged. Scholars expounding the Latin writings of Greek, Arab, and Hebrew authors attracted crowds of followers and pupils. Schools were formed, as old documents prove, and in particular a school of medical studies was founded. The first important document in this regard is dated 1137. In it a certain Adelbert of Mainz is mentioned, who, after having travelled extensively through Europe in search of learning, came to Montpellier in that year to study medicine. Later he became renowned as Bishop Adelbert II of Mainz. It goes without saying that in a town where numerous pilgrims, not a few of whom were ill, found shelter, rest, and care for a few days, doctors from the Occident and the Orient came to take care of the sick and to pass on their knowledge of medicine. Jews and Arabs in particular, translating from ancient writings, passed their knowledge on to a rapidly growing number of students pouring into Montpellier from Italy, Spain, the lands along the Rhine and Danube, from England and all parts of France.

The "Stone-Pine Tower," remnant of the medieval town fortifications. In it the Municipal Archives

Whereas the renowned Montpellier medical treatise, the "Livre de la guérison de Montpellier" seems to go back to the year 1020, the first statutes of the Medical School of Montpellier are dated 1220. With that, the city can claim to house the oldest medical school in the world within its walls. Surely the atmosphere of tolerance characterizing teaching activities here and allowing people from differing faiths and countries to work together was an important factor in the rapidly spreading good reputation of this medical school. This is documented in the Charter issued in 1181 by the ruler of Montpellier, Guilhem VIII, at the behest of the Bishop of Maguelone, Jean de Montlaur; it assures "every person, regardless of nationality and origin" the right to "teach medicine in Montpellier in complete freedom, to instruct there without fear of the slightest impediments." Right in the middle of town, where today the street of the "Ecole de Pharmacie" is, the Medical School had its first quarters. In this section of town were also the "Collèges," such as the "Collège de Mende" (also called the 'College of the Twelve Physicians'), which was reserved for students coming from this diocese, the "Collège de Gérone," which was supported by the city of Gerona (Spain), the Collège of the Pope, and that of the King. Moreover, the town had sizable hospitals, the St. Lazare and St. Eloi. Famous names of medical history taught for a time at the Medical School, for example Gui de Chauliac, whose book "The Master of Surgery" was a classic for about 400 years, not only in the field of surgery, but even more so in anatomy.

In the middle of the 12th century the schools of law and theology had their beginnings in Montpellier. Under the influence of jurists from Italy – Placentino, for example – there was a renaissance of Roman law. As a young student in Montpellier, Guillaume de Nogaret drew up his theory of a "lay monarchy," which he later read before King Philip the Fair. Nicholas IV's Papal Bull of October 26, 1289 then stipulated that the schools in Montpellier, the faculties of medicine, law, and the arts, be combined to form a university or *studium generale*.

Under the influence of Alain of Montpellier, better known as Alain of Lille, the study of theology seems to have developed at the same time, although a regular theological faculty did not come into existence until the 14th century. Thus, already at an early stage, a community of teachers and students with a legal foundation – a university, in a word – existed at that "locus Montispessulani, celebris plurimum et famosus, aptus valde pro studio," in that place of Montpellier, that is widely renowned and superbly suited to study, as the University *cartulaire* tells us. The benevolence and favours of the popes of Avignon contributed to the further propitious growth of the University of Montpellier, as did the demise of the University of Salerno and the decline of Paris during the Hundred Years' War.

Montpellier was now an influential, flourishing city of arts and sciences, which Jacques I of Aragon called "una de melioribus villis totius mundi," one of the best towns in the whole world. It had about ten thousand houses and fifty thousand inhabitants. Beyond the town fortifications new suburbs were built,

*Entrance to the Medical Faculty
with the statue of François Lapeyronie (1678–1747),
the co-founder of the Academy of Surgery
and First Surgeon of Louis XV*

which were surrounded by a palisade five miles long. In the many monasteries and on the Isle of Maguelone the needy, destitute, and the ill were readily taken in and cared for.

Epidemics and Economic Crises

In marked contrast to this period of ascent, of economic development and the flourishing of all aspects of social and intellectual life, the period between 1348 and 1460 was characterized by economic decline, political crises, epidemics, and famines in the Languedoc and Montpellier. Robber bands made the countryside unsafe. The undernourished masses were easy prey for all kinds of epidemics. In the spring of 1348 the Black Plague made its way to the Languedoc from Italy. The catastrophic results of this epidemic can best be exemplified in a town like Montpellier. Of the 140 monks of the Monastery of the Predicants, only seven survived, of the twelve consuls, only two; overall, Montpellier lost two thirds of its inhabitants.

According to a contemporary document, mortality was so high in the Provence and Languedoc that barely one sixth of the population survived. Overburdened by royal taxes, commerce and the economy were ruined, leading to rebellions and even conditions bordering on revolution. On the evening of October 25, 1379, for example, royal emissaries sent to Montpellier to collect taxes were massacred by the aroused populace. The people's fury went as far as veritable bloodlust: they even ate the "victims' christened flesh." The effects of the

Hundred Years' War only worsened an already bad situation. In 1355 the Anglo-Gascon army of the "Black Prince" laid waste to vast areas of the Languedoc. After the murder of Louis of Orléans, insecurity only increased, effectively paralyzing economic activity. Bands of pillagers and highway robbers still roamed the countryside of the Languedoc, which was in a state of anarchic dissolution. It was only in the period after 1420 that a gradual calming and securing of conditions set in, after Charles VII entered Toulouse and conceded the establishment of a parliament and a reduction in taxes. These wise concessions had far-reaching effects indeed. From then on the Languedoc identified its fate with that of the French royal house and contributed money and men to the military enterprises of Charles VII and Joan of Arc.

During the year 1367 one of the great reformers of the Church and a benefactor of the town, Pope Urban V, came to Montpellier for an extended stay. The city has him to thank for the founding of the College of the Twelve Physicians, the College of St. Benedict, and the Monastery of St. Benedict. This important pope, who hailed from the Gévaudan, also founded the universities of Cracow, Vienna, and Geneva and supported the University of Montpellier with lasting effect.

However, not all aspects of life in the towns were as bleak as the terrible conditions and precarious situation of the region and its inhabitants would lead one to suspect. In the face of the constant threat of sudden death, of fear and crisis, a bittersweet lust for life, for enjoyment, and celebration developed. Documents of the time prove that the people of Montpellier also took advantage of every opportunity for amusement and exuberant celebration. Troupes of actors and dancers came through the town, performing in public squares, especially the Place de la Canourgue in the middle of town.

When the Nuremberg physician Münzer came to Montpellier on September 15, 1494, probably on an information mission for the Hapsburg Emperor Maximilian, he compared the "ancient and noble city" with his native city of Nuremberg and admired the Chapel of the Holy Virgin and the treasures of the Monastery of St. Benedict.

Jacques Cœur in Montpellier

In the midst of this period of decadence Montpellier had one fortunate event to record, which would considerably influence the town's further development. Around 1440 the powerful financier of the French royal house, the businessman and merchant Jacques Cœur, settled in Montpellier to establish the centre of his business empire there. He found the opportunity favourable for establishing himself in Montpellier, as the city had a good reputation in Europe, had preserved its intellectual attractiveness, and maintained very good relations with the Arabs. Through his branch offices spread throughout Europe, he imported English and Norman cloth, fabrics from Holland, jewels from Germany, and, with his galleys, spices, sugar, cotton, and silk from the Levant.

The whole section of town pressed in between Rue de la Loge and Rue Jacques Cœur owes its origin to the building activity of this rich merchant, who set up his depots here and had a sumptuous palace built. This is the beautiful, stately palace known today as the Hôtel des Trésoriers de France, which was acquired by its namesakes in 1632 and remodelled to its present state. In particulars of the building, such as the medieval pointed-arch vaults, the masterly hand of the man who had it built may still be discerned today.

The multifarious activities of Jacques Cœur, which included maintaining trade relations with the Levant and Egypt with his own fleet of twelve ships, enlivened and stimulated the town's economic life as a whole for a considerable period of time. With a handsome sum of 2,000 livres he put up the money for the splendid Merchants' Lodge, a project that had long been planned by Consuls and merchants, but for which there had been no funds. This lodge had two halls, one above the other, decorated with elegant tapestries; in one of them, the dispensation of justice took place, with the other being the place of trade. It was located on the present-day Place Jean-Jaurès until the 18th century, when it was torn down, and by now of course it has vanished completely. Jacques Cœur left Montpellier after eight successful years, moving the centre of his business to Marseille. Its harbour enabled the city to become a rapidly prospering commercial city, whereas the harbours in the Languedoc had lost importance due to increasing shallowness from sand washed in from the sea. The Montpellierans never forgave him for this "treason." Thus ended a relatively short episode of economic upswing in the town in the 15th century, which was largely due to the outstanding personality of a single highly capable merchant.

There was a new addition to academic life in this period: the founding of a Theological University by Pope Martin V in 1421. In the centuries before there had been theological instruction by the religious orders, particularly the Dominicans. Now a statute attached it to the Faculty of Law. Its significance may be fairly doubted, however, as it was under the constant vigilance of the Inquisition and was unable to prevent the spread of Protestantism in Montpellier.

Montpellier During the Religious Wars

In the Languedoc, where trade routes from all points of the compass and intellectual influences from throughout Europe and the Orient converged, where, however, for centuries no fundamental monastic reform had taken place, where priests, monks, and clerical rule often gave cause for scandal, and where famine, epidemics and desperation were not unknown, new ideas had always fallen on fertile ground. Although for various reasons neither Catharist heresy nor Albigensian Crusade had greatly affected the town of Montpellier, it was all the more involved in the religious wars between Calvinists and Catholics lasting from 1561 to 1622; they fundamentally influenced and changed the intellectual life – and the outward appearance – of the medieval town.

The cosmopolitan university city which had welcomed within its walls humanistic scholars and students coming from afar, came under the influence of the ideas of the Reformation at an early stage, from 1524/25. The first Lutherans, who had come via the Rhône valley, began preaching in 1530 in the Cevennes and in the city. They quickly gathered a growing number of followers whose protests were primarily addressed to the established order, against abuses in religious life, against royal absolutism imposed by Paris, and against the central government, which was a great burden to the region and which was not providing any help for the Languedoc's regional problems. It was grievances such as these that provided fertile soil for the new doctrine. And not the least effect of the Lutheran "infection" was the considerable number of students who came from various regions of Germany and Switzerland, bringing the new ideas in their baggage and taking an active part in the town's social and cultural life.

But what was the social, economic, and political situation in Montpellier at the beginning of the 16th century? The town's affairs lay in the hands of the six Consuls and the advisory Council of the 24 "Scholars." Royal authority was wielded by the town's governor, who had jurisdictional and administrative powers. Economically it was in a relatively good position during the first half of this century, as the plague and other epidemics were receding throughout the Languedoc and immigration was increasing the population. At the beginning of the century a considerable number of Spanish Jews who had converted to Catholicism ("Marranos") came to Montpellier. The upper class became increasingly bilingual, i. e., besides the *langue d'oc,* people spoke and wrote in French, too. A result of this change was that the writings and pamphlets propagating the Reformation were in the new *lingua franca,* French. In spite of the reforms initiated by many religious orders, such as the Frères Precheurs, the Frères Mineurs, the Augustines, or the Dominicans, there was little respect for the clergy, and the people took an increasingly critical view of them.

Events followed each other fast and furiously. Hostile confrontations took place between Catholics and Calvinists, erupting at times in violence. In 1560 a pastor from Nîmes founded the Reformed Church of Montpellier. In the same year the Protestants of the city staged a protest against the executions following the abortive Conspiracy of Amboise. The old shrine of Notre-Dame-des-Tables was desecrated and then turned into a Protestant temple. The Abbey of St. Benoît, a masterpiece of the 14th century built by Pope Urban V, was almost totally flattened. Everywhere in the region, iconoclasts stormed the churches in blind rage.

There was a brief pause in this religious war during the reign of Henri IV, King of France and Navarre, from the Edict of Nantes (1598) to the ruler's death (1610). This period of peace allowed the Huguenots to consolidate their power in the city and to found a Protestant university there. What is striking is how in this half century of religious upheaval and confrontation, the town's commercial, cultural, and social life continued to run its course apparently without any great hitch. Provisions of foodstuffs for the populace were sufficient. On the cultural and intellectual plane, in particular, as in the academic sphere, there was undisturbed activity and tremendous development, as witnessed by the vivid descriptions in the diaries of the Swiss medical students Felix and Thomas Platter. Italian and French theatre troupes performed in Montpellier, where until before the wars the people had for the most part enjoyed popular, naïve, or bawdy spectacles. This calmer period saw the founding and growth of the Botanical Gardens and the expansion of the Medical Faculty.

But this peaceful coexistence of the two religions was only to last a short while. Following the Edict of 1617 restoring the state religion in the Béarn, the Protestant General Assembly of La Rochelle resolved to recruit an army under the command of the Duke of Rohan. He was given the title of a General of the Reformed Churches in the Provinces of Languedoc and Haute Guyenne and of Governor of Montpellier, which had by this time advanced to one of the most important Protestant bastions. As did the other fortified towns, Montpellier endured several months of siege by the royal army led by Louis XIII himself. On October 18, 1622 resistance collapsed, the fortress fell, and Louis XIII marched into the town with cannons thundering, hailed by great throngs of people shouting "Long live the King and mercy."

Louis XIII and his minister Richelieu would not tolerate a state within the state. At the suggestion of the military governor, the Marquis de Valançay, the town's political council petitioned the King to build a citadel, which was immediately begun. With its bulwarks, its square design, its defiant fortified walls, this mighty fortification – which can still be admired today from the vantage point of the Polygone – is a typical example of 17th-century military architecture. Although up to this time Montpellier had been a predominantly Protestant town, the dominance of the Catholic Church was now gradually restored. The revolt of the Montpellierans began to subside in 1628, when they accepted a compromise providing that at least half of the Consuls had to be Catholics.

When Louis XIV ascended the throne (1661), the repression of the Protestants was organized systematically. They had already been excluded from the office of Consul and all official administrative posts as early as 1656; in 1670 the small "Temple" had been destroyed, the large one followed in 1684. The "Director" of the Languedoc, Lamoignon de Basville, deeming himself an "irresistible missionary," organized the police surveillance of all Protestant families and introduced compulsory christening for all the newborn. In a contemporary engraving the six ways to bring heretics back to the Catholic faith are shown: the wheel, prison, flogging, the gallows, the galleys, and the stake. The executions, which were often arranged as public spectacles, took place on the former Mars Field in front of the Citadel or before the Church of Notre-Dame-des-Tables. Here Claude Brousson, a lawyer from Nîmes and a rousing preacher who became one of the greatest heroes of Protestantism in Southern France, was executed in 1697.

After the Edict of Nantes was revoked (1685), many of the wealthiest and most active Montpellier Protestants had to go into exile, which was a heavy loss to the town economically. In the same period, Basville waged a bitter war in the Cevennes: the Camisards ("the men in shirts," Huguenot peasants) or suspects were thrown into prison in the provincial capital, sent to the galleys, or they died martyrs. In the "Tower of Constancy" in Aigues-Mortes where she was imprisoned for over three decades, Marie Durand chiselled the word *résister* in a stone block. The town itself suffered terribly during this conflict. All the medieval churches except the Cathedral of St. Pierre were destroyed, entire suburbs torn down, various groups of houses left to rot.

Montpellier in the 18th Century

In the course of the 18th century, economic progress went hand in hand with innovative building activity, to which Montpellier owes splendid monumental buildings, beautiful houses and sumptuous gardens and parks. The city took on the appearance that it was to keep, all in all, until the sixties of our century. Of course, reconstruction took a long time; it took over thirty years to repair the war damages (until 1715, the year Louis XIV died). Colbert, who initiated and carried out a number of ambitious building projects, had the ingenious Pierre-Paul Riquet build the Canal du Midi (between 1666 and 1681), an undertaking of spectacular dimensions at the time. In order to provide the canal with access to the Mediterranean, the cornerstone for the construction of the harbour of Sète was laid on July 29, 1666. Montpellier profited from the large-scale capital transactions generated by this building activity. The banks were busy. The big bankers, most of them from Huguenot families, had adapted to the new political and economic conditions and, thanks to their wealth, played an important social and political role.

But this favourable economic development was also due to the growth and expansion of manufacturing. Montpellier had remained a city renowned for its cloth. Changes in fashion such as the introduction of silk stockings were a boon to the textile industry. Montpellier's handkerchief production took control of the markets, as "the fashion of taking snuff makes a person use ten times more handkerchiefs than usual." Moreover, textile enterprises in the valleys of the Cevennes were controlled from Montpellier. On the cultural level, still a privileged sphere of the office-holding elite and the magistrates, there were also new impulses. Two councillors of the audit authority, François-Xavier Bon and François de Plantade, founded the Royal Academy of Sciences in 1706. The Bishop of Montpellier, Colbert, noblemen, jurists, and physicians joined the newly formed society. Even though the members' scholarly works were on the conventional side (a description of deformed foetuses, for example, or the observation of eclipses), the circle of academy members took a keen interest in the philosophical developments of the 18th century. But an oppressive atmosphere of intolerance was still predominant otherwise. There was still persecution and the execution of Protestants continued. They retreated more and more into the impassable wilderness of the Garrigue and the Cevennes to worship as they pleased. The new spirit of enlightenment didn't assert itself until 1770, with the liberation of the last prisoners from the "Tower of Constancy" in Aigues-Mortes.

The newly won state of peace, prestige, and wealth was expressed in an impressive upswing of monumental and stately urban architecture which may fairly be referred to as the "Montpellier Style." Gifted architects such as Daviler or the "dynasty" of the Montpellierans, Giral and Donnat, gave the city's appearance new dimensions by designing large parks and handsome urban palaces *(hôtels)*.

The outstanding characteristic of these *hôtels particuliers,* built by wealthy burghers and the landed gentry, is their surprising variety of detail. Through usually sparsely decorated portals one steps in from the narrow street to bright, richly and imaginatively ornamented courtyards. Monumental stairways with beautiful wrought-iron bannisters or huge marble balustrades lead from these courtyards to living quarters and reception rooms. In this way, the nobility, financiers, or landowners of the 18th century provided themselves with a private, protected refuge which discreetly concealed its comforts, luxury, and wealth. Over 100 of these *hôtels* can be found dispersed throughout the city's historic centre. In this period of prosperity, the *folies,* pretty 18th-century country homes, were also built in the surrounding countryside, nestled in parks providing plentiful shade, as well as seignorial residences and palaces, such as "La Piscine", built for Richer de Belleval; the "Château d'O" on the road to Grabels, with its large artificial pond and its stage-like perspectives, which is used today by the General Council for representation purposes; the "Château de la Mogère", overlooking the plain towards Mauguio; or "La Mosson," built by Giral.

The urban planners of the 18th century deserve praise for including spacious green zones in the city. After the Esplanades had been built, providing shade towards the East, the largest project of the 18th century – the construction of the Peyrou – was begun under the architect Daviler. Here, a masterpiece of Montpellier's architecture would be achieved. A monumental bridge connected the spacious terraced plot to the city, replacing the old drawbridge formerly crossing the moat. At the edge of the city's old centre, Daviler built the Arch of Triumph in honour of Louis XIV, commemorating his military successes, the building of the "Channel of the Two Seas," and the revoking of the Edict of Nantes, thus permanently documenting architecturally that royal absolutism and the Roman Catholic Church had maintained the upper hand over the city in a series of long drawn-out conflicts. An equestrian statue of Louis XIV towers over the centre of the gardens. The beautiful symmetry of the park is underscored by the quaint harmoniously proportioned water tower built by Giral in 1770. There the *arceaux,* the aqueduct, built by the engineer Pitot between 1753 and 1765 and over half a mile long, discharges the water it brings to the city from the St. Clément spring.

Chapel of the General Hospital (1751–1756), built by Jean Giral, the most elegant of Montpellier's classical churches

The population increased towards the end of the 17th century, which came to a close in peace and prosperity, resulting in the city's expansion beyond the boundaries of the medieval fortifications. New suburbs grew along the roads leading into the city: the Faubourg of Lattes, the Faubourg St. Guilhem, or the Faubourg St. Jaumes. On the eve of the Revolution, Montpellier had indisputably become the capital of the region thanks to its institutions – the university, its courts, banks, and commercial centre – and it wielded its cultural, administrative, and economic influence over the entire area of the lower Languedoc.

Montpellier in the Revolutionary Period

The revolutionary events of 1789 were hailed with enthusiasm in Montpellier. As early as August 18, 1789, citizens of the city had founded the "Légion de Montpellier," the first version of the national militia *(garde nationale)*. After the garrison stationed in the Citadel laid down its arms on May 1, 1790, a Jacobin Club, the "Society of the Friends of the Constitution," was formed in the same year; it was probably one of the first to demand the proclamation of the Republic. In 1790–92 commerce and manufacturing thrived thanks to the abolition of domestic excise taxes and bridge tolls, but also due to profiteering by merchants who bought up church and state property. After the first wave of enthusiasm passed, political dissent grew, leading to unrest and uprisings in 1793. Moreover, the crash in value of the *assignats,* the termination of trade relations with Spain, and the interruption of maritime commerce ruined Montpellier's economy. So when Napoleon's *coup d'état* of the 18th of Brumaire came along, Montpellier celebrated with a solemn Te Deum.

Montpellier's involvement in the Revolution is probably best illustrated by the lives of two natives of the city who were important in determining its course. One was Pierre Joseph Cambon (1756–1820), of whom the historian Michelet has written with unbounded admiration. He came from a wealthy and respected family of Languedoc cloth merchants and founded the "Society of the Friends of Equality" in Montpellier, which was associated with the Jacobins in Paris. After he was elected to the Legislative Assembly, he managed the difficult financial matters of the Revolution with great skill. The other outstanding figure on the revolutionary stage was Jean Jacques Cambacérès (1753–1824). Before becoming a delegate to the National Convention, he was a councillor in Montpellier's audit authority and President of the Penal Court of Hérault. He was just as skilled as Cambon in maneuvering in revolutionary politics, without compromising himself with too great concessions either to the right or the left. Like his compatriot Cambon, he survived the Reign of Terror. The Constitution of the Year VIII of the Revolution (Dec. 24, 1799) named him as one of the three Consuls. He became the most influential adviser of Napoleon, who finally appointed him Archchancellor of the Empire.

After the Revolution of 1789, it is remarkable how unperturbed Montpellier survived the other revolutionary unrest of the 19th century. Uprisings, civil wars, changes of government, and economic crises had only a very limited effect on the calm progress of business and an introspective way of life. The Revolution had been enthusiastically hailed at the fall of the Citadel; the garrison had surrendered without a fight. Under the Directorate, the city went through a siege once more. But Napoleon's *coup d'état* of the 18th of Brumaire (Nov. 9, 1799) quickly restored the old order. During the Restoration the city was so thoroughly purged that the prisons were overcrowded. The city's last moments of unrest occurred when the monarchy was restored; but even the Revolution of 1830 was met here with nearly complete calm, marred only slightly by a few replacements in the Prefecture and the city government.

The Nineteenth Century

Due to the administrative changes in the post-revolutionary years, Montpellier lost its function as the administrative centre and capital of France's largest province and was demoted to being simply the capital of a "department." However, the crucial occurrence in the first decades of the 19th century was the expansion of viticulture and the development of a bonafide enology and wine industry, influenced by the writings of professors Chaptal and Adam. A boldly expansive trade in wine and spirits brought new economic energy to the city and led to the building of one of the first French railroad lines. On June 9, 1839 the railroad connecting Montpellier with Sète was inaugurated, opening a rapid connection to the seaport. One year later, the neo-classical railroad station was built, whose festooned façade reinforced by columns still welcomes travellers today.

Montpellier had become a bustling city of well-to-do *bourgeois*. In mid-century, local textile manufacturing had declined; it had been unable to keep pace with the mechanized competition in the North. For this reason, a proletariat didn't form in Montpellier, so that the great social movements and migrations of that century only marginally affected life in the city. The disappearance of the textile industry went hand in hand with another important development of lasting consequence: the end of large-scale commercial transactions. Gradually, the economy came to be dominated by viticulture and the wine trade.

In this quiet century, too, the building projects realized on a grand scale were eloquent testimony of the city's economic well-being. Under the leadership of capable mayors, who were also good businessmen, such as Granier, Castelnau, and Pagézy, large-scale urban projects were begun to meet the demands dictated by the times and the population increase: the city walls were removed;

streets built joining the suburbs to the city's centre; neglected and run-down neighbourhoods were revamped; other streets were broadened such as those of St. Guilhem, Maguelone, and de la Loge. But the most important – and controversial – project was the "Champs Elysées" of Montpellier, the present-day Rue Foch (formerly Rue Impériale, later Rue Nationale), which impassioned resistance prevented from being completed until 1886 and which provides the present grand perspective from the Square of the Martyrs of the Resistance past the Arch of Triumph to the Peyrou.

The 19th century also witnessed the birth of a new kind of house. The lordly *hôtel particulier* is replaced by bourgeois houses with flats, which still lay claim to stateliness. This type of house, a status symbol of the emerging bourgeois class, was built along the broadened streets as a three-story building, with the ground floor reserved for shops. The richly decorated and sometimes overdone façades, on which the entire decorative repertoire of Renaissance and Classicism can be found, with Atlases, caryatids, garlands, and smiling women's heads, demonstrated the wealth of their owners. This bourgeois century displays a predilection for the theatre and the theatrical gesture. Thus, the owner of house no. 6 Rue Boussairolles had a miniature of the staircase of the Paris opera made in the same Baroque marble splendour – a veritable jewel of urban architecture. Now it is the bourgeoisie that decides the fate of the city, and they lay claim to the central, bright neighbourhoods around Rue Foch and the Place de la Comédie for their dwellings, abandoning the neglected areas of St. Roch and Valfère in the historic centre to the less well-to-do. Small industry is on the increase in the suburbs: mechanics and tanners at Pont Juvénal, coopers along the Cours Gambetta; whereas the Faubourg Boutonnet preserved its rural character. The industrialization which changed the physiognomy of many European cities at the mid-century mark passed Montpellier by. At the end of the century, Montpellier was completely underindustrialized, with 15 % of its work force employed in manufacturing in 1891, as compared to 75 % in the service trades. With the founding of the National Institute of Agriculture, the insights of modern agronomy are made available to the landed bourgeoisie. But it couldn't prevent the already apparent structural crisis of viticulture leading to a prolonged stagnation of the city's economy at the beginning of the 20th century, with effects lasting up to the fifties.

This period of consolidation, during which the city was little affected by political upheaval and social unrest, saw cultural and academic life take a favourable turn. True to its international traditions, the university admitted students, professors, and physicians from throughout Europe who had been driven from their homes by political unrest. "Germany has also sent a contingent. Among students at the Medical School, the blond faces stand out; talking to them, one learns that they are students from the Palatinate or Baden, refugees taking advantage of the one faculty the University has and thus willy-nilly studying medicine. They have predecessors in this fate: for in rural areas

Building in the Lonjon Passage (1898). Because of its form and the four "portholes," the turret is also referred to as "The Diver"

there are German doctors whom the late lamented Frankfurt incident also drove to Montpellier and into the arms of medicine." This bit of news is from the pen of the Austrian travel writer Moritz Hartmann who, himself a political refugee, gives a charming and informative portrait of social life in the city around the middle of the 19th century in his "Diary of a Journey through the Languedoc and Provence." Absolutely penniless and fleeing after the failure of the German Revolution of 1848, he found a hospitable reception at the hands of the artist and writer François Sabatier in his palace, Latour de Farges, about 18 miles from Montpellier. From there – he stayed from May to October, 1851 – he made excursions into the Languedoc and to Montpellier. His sympathetic and vivid descriptions of the everyday life and habits of the townspeople, of cultural events, and university·life constitute an interesting contemporary document.

Montpellier from 1900 to 1960

The first half of this century, which had seen tremendous upheaval and social and economic structural changes in central European regions as a result of the two World Wars, was a period of stagnation in Montpellier. The city survived both wars without destruction of its buildings, thus leaving the building plan which had evolved in the 18th and 19th centuries largely intact. New buildings worthy of note were built by the architect Edmond Leenhardt (1870–1950). He was the son of one of the most prominent Protestant families of Montpellier and returned home after studying at the School of Fine Arts in Paris. Here he was an active builder and was a major force in the city's architecture of the first three decades of this century. The villas and country homes of well-to-do families unmistakably bear his stamp. Their main features are a harmonic combination of hand-hewn natural-stone blocks with overhanging wooden roofing, often decorated by a frieze. There is a touch of romantic enchantment to these architectural creations; the discreetly placed flowery Art Nouveau ornaments on façades, balconies, and portals fit in with the Mediterranean vegetation of the gardens surrounding them. The degree to which Leenhardt imprinted his stamp on the city in these years is clearly visible when viewing the villas which were built on Avenue de Lodève. Take, for example, the villa "Les Chardons" ('The Thistles'), which serves today as the residence of the Rector of the Academy, or the villa next to it, "Harmonie," built for a famous singer of that time, Emma Calvé. Of the many large-scale projects carried out since 1915 which still give the city's appearance its characteristic stamp, the building of the Banque Nationale de Paris on Rue Maguelone and the neo-Gothic Bouisson Betrand Institute opposite the entrance to the Medical Faculty should be mentioned. Edmond Leenhardt was also commissioned by Patric Geddes to build an enlarged 'College of Scots' ("Collège des Ecossais"). This large and important institution in Montpellier's cultural history was erected on the 'Plain of the Four Lords' ("Plan des quatre Seigneurs") overlooking the city from the North, with one of the most breathtaking views of the city and the coast.

At the beginning of the century Montpellier had 74,000 inhabitants; by 1954, the population was 97,500. The city's slow growth is primarily due to the structural crisis in the economy of the entire region of the Languedoc. In a city whose dependence on viticulture and the wine trade was so pronounced that 318 people in the city owned vineyards in 1910, the permanent crisis of the wine business had to have adverse effects. Overproduction and monetary and real-estate speculation had led to a first crisis, beginning in 1850. The second crisis – this time a biological one – had a much greater impact on the area: it was infested by the vine louse *(phylloxera)*. The new disease of the vines caused by this pest, which was first discovered in the Department of Gard in 1869, spread rapidly from the East towards the West. By 1876, one third of the vineyards around Montpellier were already completely destroyed. There were two effective cures to the disease: putting the vineyards under water or grafting French grapevines onto American vine stems which were resistant to the vine louse. The third crisis was a colonialist/mercantile one; it came when mass-produced wine was imported by French settlers in Algeria via the port of Sète. The situation was aggravated by the flooding of the market with adulterated and artificial wines, which were extremely detrimental to the reputation of the Languedoc.

This desperate situation, particularly for the small vintners, led to large vintner demonstrations in 1907, the biggest of which took place in Montpellier on June 9, 1907, with about 600,000 demonstrators taking part. The Bishop of Montpellier, Cabrières, who was known for his social commitment, opened the portals of the Cathedral to afford a haven to the demonstrators.

During the first half of the century, the six large cities of the southwestern rim of France, Avignon, Nîmes, Montpellier, Béziers, Carcassone, and Perpignan, competed with each other in the economic sector whenever they could, and none was able to gain predominance. Montpellier remained the administrative centre of the Languedoc and, thanks to the University, clinics, and other institutions of higher learning, its intellectual centre. But compared to other cities in France which underwent an economic and population boom in the fifties, Montpellier remained within the boundaries it had had at the end of the 19th century. The beginning of a new era of modernization, dynamism, and expansion didn't come until the beginning of the sixties.

And so the essentially nineteenth-century physiognomy of Montpellier remained virtually unchanged in the first half of this century. Nor did the last war bring any major transformations. Life in the renowned university town continued at a leisurely pace; here, as in other cities of the Languedoc, the rhythm of urban life was shaped by the rhythms of the surrounding countryside. Streetcars with open platforms rumbled unhurriedly across the Place de la Comédie with passengers calling out to greet passers-by. Where the modern building complex known as Le Triangle stands today, you could find –

"La Bulle," a familiar figure to the Montpellierans

well into the sixties – the old Palavas Station. From here a little steam train, immortalized by caricaturists and poets, used to set out for the seaside.

The writer Valéry Larboud, for whom Montpellier was one of the secret capitals of France, has commemorated the city of those years in the following evocative description: "No English spa without its Montpelier Road or Montpelier Street, written here with one 'l'. Eloquent testimony to the fame of Montpellier as a centre of medicine and as a city in which to spend the winter. In Russian literature Montpellier must have its rightful place alongside San Remo, Nizza, or Vichy. It would be interesting to pursue this, to follow these very real traces of the links between the University of Montpellier and Russian intellectual life. Lonely streets in springlike twilight. Gliding along in an open landau carriage, through broad white streets leading to white and graceful suburbs, walls on either side behind which avenues of yews and cypresses rise up. Thick dust carpets the road without a sidewalk; heavy yet fine dust which the carriage wheels fail to whirl up. Above the tops of the cypresses the first star."

The Horse Market under the "Arceaux"

Next double spread:
The Opera, built by Cassien-Bernard,
inaugurated on October 1, 1888
with a production of "Les Huguenottes"
by Giacomo Meyerbeer. On the right, the
Fountain of the Three Graces (1776)
by the sculptor Etienne d'Antoine

53

*The most important medical library
in the French provinces, also containing
manuscripts of the 8th and 9th centuries*

Façade of the Faculty of Medicine;
until the 14th century it was a Benedictine
monastery, then the bishop's seat from the
16th to 18th centuries

*The "Arceaux:" an aqueduct over half
a mile long and 70 ft. high, built from 1753
to 1764 by the hydraulics engineer Pitot*

"La Babote," along with the "Stone-pine Tower" one of the few remnants left of the original 25 towers encircling Montpellier seven centuries ago

*Rue Joubert. The English poet
Edward Young, father of Narcissa,
lived in house no. 2 in 1742*

*Rue du Bras-de-Fer. Its name is derived
from a sign depicting an iron arm*

Rue de l'Ancien Courrier,
one of the first pedestrian zones

On the Boulevard Jeu-de-Paume

Drug store on Place Castellane

Place Saint-Roch

The Place de la Comédie viewed from the Esplanade

The Esplanade, the connecting link between the Place de la Comédie und the Corum

The Botanical Gardens

Slowly, through the stony, winding little streets of this ancient city, we will go to this old garden to which all the people descend towards evening, laden with thoughts and cares, to speak their monologues.

Paul Valéry

Below the Peyrou, very near the old Medical School from which they are separated today by the busy Boulevard Henri IV, the Botanical Gardens are situated in a hollow. Their origins are intimately connected with the medieval history of the University, particularly with its Medical School.

The visitor would do well to choose a warm morning in the early summer for his visit, when the soil and plants are still breathing the maritime dampness of the preceding night, and the transparent blue of the Mediterranean sky extends above the trees. Entering by the wrought-iron gate, whose inscription "University of Montpellier" identifies this ordered universe of vegetation as a university domain, one suddenly finds oneself in a shady realm of plants unrivalled for its variety. Here, spread out before the visitor, is everything the karstic Garrigue, the dunes of the coast, the barren Cevennes, the temperate zones and even the tropics are known for. The renowned biologist Hervé Harant, Director of the Gardens for many years, put it this way, "Primarily, a botanical garden must afford a total view of natural history." Its main attractions include the *Phillirea latifolia,* probably the oldest tree in the Gardens, going back to the time of their founding. But the imposing row of towering cypresses are also impressive, as are the mighty Micocouliers *(Celtis australis),* celebrated in the poems of the Provençal poet Mistral, not to mention the chestnut oak, the wide-branched Siberian elm *(Zelkova),* or the massive, gnarled Himalayan cedar . . .

But in this world of plants, the visitor should concentrate on the subtle sensations of scents. In the mild humidity-sated air, the striking aromas of thyme and rosemary are mixed with the sweetness of witch hazel and lavender; here we find the balsamic scents of fennel, origanum, sweet Mary, and basil; over there is the tangy, swampy smell of tamarisk, the characteristic tree of the swampy coastal strip. From time to time a sweet scent of roses hidden somewhere in the lush green wafts by, full of presentiment. On these few acres of nature, which have been cared for for centuries, the spicy, intoxicating scents of the aridly karstic Garrigue and the foothills of the Cevennes so rich in herbs form a symbiosis with the tangy salt- and iodine-rich emanations of the swampy coast.

Passing through a stone archway, the visitor is suprised to find himself in a little forest of laurel and cypress, in the realm of legend. He stands before a simple gravestone with the inscription "Narcissæ placandis manibus" ('To the mourning survivors of Narcissa'). Here the beautiful stepdaughter of the English poet Edward Young, Narcissa, is said to have found her final resting place after

The Botanical Gardens, founded in 1593 by Richer de Belleval. André Gide and Paul Valéry liked to have long talks here

dying at the tender age of sixteen. The father purportedly picked out this peaceful, solemn burial place secretly, under cover of darkness. One can't help thinking of Malherbe's line, "And, rose, it lived as roses live, for the space of a morning."

From very early on, probably as far back as the mid-16th century, a devotion of botany was part of medical studies, as shown by the plant collecting of the illustrious Dr. Nostradamus. A convincing representative of the European spirit is the botanist Charles de l'Ecluse, who, before coming to Montpellier, had studied philosophy in Marburg and theology in Wittenberg under Melanchthon. In this period the students of the Medical School already had a little garden of European repute. In 1593 King Henri IV commissioned Pierre Richer de Belleval to begin with a Botanical Garden in Montpellier. Although this original garden was destroyed several times during the course of the religious wars, Richer de Belleval always endeavoured to expand on what he had begun. Particularly felicitous was the appointment of Pierre Magnol (for whom the magnolia is named) to teach botany. After publishing "Botanicum monspeliense" and "Prodromus historiæ generalis plantarum," he compiled an interesting description of the Botanical Gardens, "Hortus Regius Monspelliensis" (1697). It is impossible to list all the directors here; they were all responsible for continuing research in these Botanical Gardens in the course of the centuries. At any rate, Charles Martin (1851–1879), who is credited with founding the School of Medical Plants, should be mentioned, as should Jules-Emile Planchon, who was prominent in the fight against *Phylloxera* (the vine louse), and Charles Flahault, the founder of the Botanical Institute. His monument is at the northern end of the Gardens, but since 1949 there has also been one to Richer de Belleval, sculpted by Guére, very near the Palais académique, which is adorned with one of the most beautiful wisterias in France, the *Wisteria sirensis*. But in the middle of the Gardens a stone monument commemorates the Montpellieran master of medicine, the mighty mocker, the creator of Gargantua and Pantagruel, the outstanding mind of his time – François Rabelais.

However, you can no longer "descend to the Gardens in the evening," as Paul Valéry once did. As a domain of the University, it is unfortunately closed not only in the evening, but also on Saturday afternoons and Sundays and holidays.

Rabelais

It is better to write of laughter than of tears, because laughter is what is typical of man
(Gargantua)

Even today, a newly graduated doctor of medicine is draped with the red doctor's robe that François Rabelais wore after passing his examination in the "Hall of Acts" of the Medical School of Montpellier.

On September 1, 1530 François Rabelais, already a mature man of 40, enrolled as a student of medicine at the University of Montpellier. The man who officially enrolled him for the Faculty was none other than Guillaume Rondelet, who later became a professor, the model for Rondibilis in Rabelais' work. Rabelais' high cultivation must have made a lasting impression on his teachers, for the renowned professor of medicine Jean Schyron already nominated him for the bachelor's examination on December 1 of that year, which he passed brilliantly. To attain higher degrees Rabelais gave a course of lectures on the aphorisms of Hippocrates from April to June 1531. In February 1532, the year "Pantagruel" was published in Lyon, he took his examination for the "licentiate." After extensive travels, to Rome and elsewhere, he was admitted to an *actus triumphalis* at the University of Montpellier, i. e., to a doctoral examination. On passing it, the insignia of his degree were presented to him in a ceremony in the Church of Saint Firmin: he was given the square black-linen cap, the ring, the golden belt, and the book of Hippocrates. After that he stayed for a time in Montpellier, as dictated by tradition, to let the students profit from the knowledge he had acquired. We know that a "Franciscus Rabelaesus" was present at the meeting of Francis I and Charles V in July 1538 in Aigues-Mortes. Then came years of travel throughout Europe. Rabelais enjoyed the years he spent in Montpellier to the full extent his intense zest for life allowed. The Montpellier he experienced was probably the same as that described by the Swiss brothers Felix and Thomas Platter in a literary diary a few decades later: the city comprised 10,000 fires, i. e., 40,000 inhabitants. Numerous church spires towered over the city, and in the suburbs there were just as many monasteries, surrounded by gardens, vineyards, and olive groves. The city walls were two miles long, with a moat 65 feet deep, ten gates, and 25 towers. One expects to see Rabelais strolling with his friend through the narrow, winding streets around St. Guilhem and St. Firmin. He not only went for walks along the Lez, whose clear waters he extols, he also drank the healing water from the springs of Balaruc, which he says was Pantagruel's urine. He also saw the goat herds come down from the high plateaus of the Causses, for he says that Gargantua's mare's ears drooped like those of the goats from "Langueguoth."

And he is sure to have liked "this good wine of Langueguoth which grows in Mirevaulx, Canteperdix, and Frontignan," as his hero Pantagruel says, claiming it was the best of them all. Another author, who came all the way from

Bohemia to Lower Languedoc four hundred years later, erected this fine monument to the great humanist and master of mockery:

"But one doesn't feel really good and happy and serene at the Medical Faculty until one looks the Montpellieran professor by the name of Alcofribas Nasier in the eye, who is also known as Master Wag or Rabbi Lez, as well as François Rabelais. There standing before us is one of those French minds which can be named together with the best and freest of all nations. Rabelais! Like a Janus he stands between two ages, but he looks in both directions with white, smiling teeth, backwards to the dying, clumsy Gargantua, ahead to Pantagruel, the benefactor of humanity, the good man who entices all the thirsty to taste the chalice of life, knowledge – and enjoyment. Can't one see by looking at him that he had to be persecuted by monks early on? That laughing, he slipped by the stakes threatening from all sides? That while laughing he helped, healed, and uttered lofty truths? That in the end he died laughing: when the end came, he said, 'Let down the curtain, the farce is over'? Rabelais' whole life, Rabelais himself is in his entiretys but one big laugh, joyful laughter, prophetic laughter echoing through the entire 16th century, laughter for joy at the night's ending, at the day so beautifully beginning, at the newly discovered world in the West, at the rebirth of Greek antiquity and its twin sister, beauty, at the great, wonderful struggle that the Reformation was waging in all countries."

" 'Laughter is what is typical of man,' he said at the bedside in the hospital and at mankind's bedside. It is difficult to separate the hospital director Rabelais at Lyon from the Rabelais who in his books belongs to all humanity.

"What he says as the former is also true of the author of Pantagruel, of the inventor of Pantagruelism: 'A care-worn, aloof, unobliging, dissatisfied, strict, annoyed facial expression depresses the patient; but a happy, serene, obliging, open, joyful doctor's face does the patient good'." (From Moritz Hartmann, "Diary of a Journey through the Languedoc and Provence")

*The Student. Detail of the monument
to Rabelais in the Botanical Gardens*

73

The Cathedral of Saint Peter

With its massive quadruple towers and monumental nave, the Cathedral of St. Peter is not only one of the most important architectural monuments of the city, but also an eloquent witness of the church and religious history of the region. Originally conceived as a chapel of the Monastery of St. Benedict, it was made a cathedral with the transferral of the bishop's seat from Maguelone to Montpellier. Construction was begun in 1364 at the instigation of Pope Urban V. In the course of the religious wars all but the mighty nave and three of the four towers were destroyed between 1561 and 1567; the Cathedral was, however restored after the original plans at the behest of Richelieu between 1622 and 1630. The old Gothic choir was replaced in 1775 by one of a new design, and the destroyed tower was restored and a Neogothic transept with choir were added by the architect Henri Revoil in 1855–1875. The middle nave, which is 89 ft. high, is impressive for its classical symmetry and majestic simplicity. The organ, built by Jean-François l'Epine in 1776/78, harmoniously fits into the space as a whole. In one of the side chapels is the tombstone of Cardinal de Cabrières (1830–1921), who, as Bishop of Montpellier, opened the Cathedral as a haven for the demonstrating vintners during the largest vintner protest in the history of France, on June 9, 1907. Even today, the Cathedral is the backdrop for great moments in Montpellier's history. High points of the celebration of the millenium of the city of Montpellier in 1986 and the seventh centennial of its University were the colourful ecumenical memorial services held in this defiant fortress of faith.

The apse of the Cathedral with its
polychrome roof and four towers

The water tower on the Peyrou, an architectural creation of Jean-Antoine Giral, completed in 1774

The water tower: "Everything is totally serene . . ." (Gaston Baissette)

The Peyrou

A tourist asking for the "Peyrou" may detect pride or even a trace of transfiguration in the face of the native of Montpellier he is asking directions of. Indeed, the western end of the city's historic centre borders on a promenade lined with plane trees which affords one of the most beautiful and inspiring views in Southern France.

After just a few steps, the many-voiced, noisy bustle of the city is forgotten, and one finds oneself in an expansive plot of terraced gardens receptive to the breeze from the sea. From here, the red-tiled roofs of the city and the surrounding countryside, interspersed with country homes nestled in its green, are at the viewer's feet. The four towers of the Cathedral are so close that it seems as though one could reach out and touch them. But let us have the travel author Moritz Hartmann go on with the description of the view; he was probably just as impressed by his promenade on the Peyrou in mid-September, 1851 as we are today: "To the North are the chalky, scorched mountains of the Cevennes with their king, the Pic St. Loup; towards the South, the smiling, blue Mediterranean Sea, which is only six miles from the city, with the green swamps on its shores and the Island of Maguelone and the ruins of the famed old church in its midst; to the West, when the weather is particularly clear, beyond the last foothills of the Cevennes, which spread their arms towards the sea, one can even see the huge tops of the Pyrenees swimming in a soft blue. When the air is mixed with the humidity from the nearby sea, the Cevennes seem to have moved so near that one feels as though one could touch the bushes and solitarily nodding alpine blossoms and boldly step into the caves and crevasses. On the Esplanade opposite the Peyrou, one can see not only the Cevennes and Pyrenees, but also the Alps with their representative, Mont Ventoux, thus greeting in one moment, with one glance, Hispania, Helvetia, *la belle France,* and, through the medium of the Mediterranean Sea, fabled Africa. A cosmopolitan heart can find nourishment here just as readily as that of a hypochondriac lost in thought on the pettiness of the realms of this world, even of this poor countryside."

After his victory at Fleurus, Louis XIV wanted to give Montpellier a garden worthy of the Sun King. Under the architect Daviler, work was begun on the monumental project in 1689. It was planned as an imposing terrace, promenade, high look-out point, a gathering place, a proud manifestation of urban power and prestige, and a permanent reminder of the royal presence. It took a hundred years, for work on the 575 × 410-ft. project was not completed until 1776 under the architect Jean-Antoine Giral. A gem of urban architecture is the charming water tower, another product of Giral's inspiration; with its idiosyn-

Stairway on the Peyrou

On the Peyrou. Equestrian statue of Louis XIV, by the sculptor Debay (1838)

cratic hexagonal style and richly decorated Corinthian columns, it is at once the vanishing point of the promenade and the connection to the municipal aqueduct. The mighty aqueduct which ends here brings water to the city from the St. Clément spring nearly 5 miles away. It is a masterpiece of construction by the hydraulic engineer Pitot (1762). The aqueduct and the boulevard beneath it are to the Montpellierans the "Arceaux," for short. Here is where the horse market takes place, where the "Pétanque" and tambourine players are at home.

But let us by no means forget the bronze Sun King Louis XIV high on his horse, a symbol of French centralism outlasting the epochs; with a commanding gesture and bold look, he seems to be issuing orders from the centre of the square. This powerful and at the same time charming equestrian statue, a masterpiece by the sculptor Debay, was erected at its present location after many quirks of fate on August 7, 1838 – to succeed a first statue by the sculptors Pierre Mazelin and Simon Hurtrelle, which had been toppled during the Revolution in 1792 – to a marked lack of enthusiasm from the townspeople.

Saint Roch

In the eastern part of the historic centre, on the corner of a house where the Vieille Aiguillerie, the Aiguillerie, and the Pila-Saint-Gély meet, an inscription can be found on a marble plaque which reads, "Here legend has it that poor Roch sat down exhausted on a bench upon returning to Montpellier and was arrested." Together with St. Firmin, St. Roch is a patron saint of the city.

He was born in about 1340 in Montpellier as the son of the merchant family Rog. After losing both parents at the age of 20, he donned his pilgrim's robe, picked up his staff, and left for Rome, taking the medieval "Cami Roumiou," the 'Pilgrims' Way,' which went through Montpellier. After a sojourn of several years in the Eternal City, his journey took him to Aquapendente and Rimini, where he miraculously healed many people suffering from plague. After having contracted the disease himself, he retired to a forest, and at the spot where he stopped, a spring issued forth to cool his fever. A dog from a nearby manor brought him his food each day. After being arrested as a spy, St. Roch is said to have died in Angera, Lombardy, in about 1379.

According to the legend, however, he returned to his native city, where he was suspected of being a spy and died in a dungeon. His grandmother is said to have recognized him on his deathbed from a red mark on his skin in the shape of a cross that he had had from youth. After the relics of the Saint were brought to Venice in 1485, his veneration rapidly spread from the Mediterranean area to Northern Europe. The cholera epidemic of 1854 in Languedoc and Montpellier brought an increase in the Saint's veneration. The Church of St. Roch was dedicated to him in 1860. In 1884 the beautiful sculpture by Baussan was placed there. The Montpellierans remember their patron saint in another place, too. On August 16, the saint's feast day, they go to his place of birth on the corner of Rue de la Loge and Rue des Trésoriers-de-France to draw water from the Well of St. Roch, which is purported to have healing powers.

Detail from a stained-glass window in the Church of St. Roch showing the city's patron saint (by master Milon)

The 230 ft. bell tower of St. Anne's (built 1866–1869)

The Museum Fabre

Like the Municipal Library, the Museum Fabre is on the spacious grounds of the former Jesuit College. To the left of the impressive façade Antoine Injalbert's beautiful sculpture "Poetry of Love in Passion and Melancholy" graces a niche in the wall. It was originally mounted on a commercial building on the Place de la Comédie in 1894, but it unleashed such a wave of moral protest that it was removed and eventually brought to the present more discreet location. Before the Museum was reorganized, the entrance was next to the Hôtel Massilian, which is to this day part of the Museum. A marble plaque notes that Molière performed here in the winter of 1654/55. Thanks to the great number and the quality of its treasures, the Fabre is one of the outstanding museums of the French provinces. Its origins go back to 1780, when the "Society of Fine Arts" established an art gallery. When insufficient funds forced its dissolution in 1787, the art works were entrusted to the Art Institute. In the wake of the French Revolution, 30 paintings stemming from the art treasures confiscated by the state were donated to Montpellier in 1802. This nucleus of the collection was first kept on Rue des Etuves and later in the Hôtel de Belleval, the future Guildhall *(Mairie)* at the Place de la Canourgue. But for this to become a museum worthy of the name, the painter François-Xavier Fabre had to come along.

Born in Montpellier on April 1, 1766 as the son of a faience painter, he was himself attracted to art, became a pupil of Couston, Vien, and David, and then went to Rome in 1787 with a scholarship of the French Academy (Académie de France). When the Revolution broke out, he decided to stay in Italy and settled in Florence, where his father and brother had already established themselves. During the many years he lived there in his middle age (1794–1825), he made two friendships which would prove to be crucial to him and to the art Montpellier would one day possess: one was with the poet Vittorio Alfieri (1749–1803) and the other with his mistress, Luise von Stolberg, Countess of Albany, widow of Charles Edward Stuart, who was called the "Young Pretender." The triangle so often described in literature developed, but this one was harmonious. Fabre was himself a recognized teacher and painter and became the preferred portrait painter of the English coming to Florence on their "grand tour." In this genre he was indeed a master. His income allowed him to amass a large collection, consisting of drawings, French landscapes of the 17th century, and Italian works which is now in the Museum Fabre.

After Alfieri's death (1803), he remained the Countess's companion until her death in 1825. He inherited not only her extensive collection of paintings, but also Alfieri's precious and voluminous library. There now being no reason to stay in Florence any longer, he decided to settle in his native city and to give it his collection of paintings and books. In January 1825, the City Council resolved to accept the offer of 224 paintings, 26 drawings, 72 etchings, and other objects of art, as well as a library of 9,000 volumes. To house this

*At the Museum Fabre in the company
of Gustave Courbet (1819–1877) and
Serge Poliakoff (1900–1969)*

acquisition, the city bought and remodelled the Hôtel Massilian, and it was officially opened on December 3, 1828. Fabre was its first Curator as well as Director of the Art Institute. He was heaped with all sorts of honours, such as the Legion of Honour, and Charles X made him a baron. He remained Curator and Director until his death in 1837.

Fabre's collection included a splendid series of works by the Italians Veronese, Caravaggio, and Carlo Dolci, and the Spaniard Ribera, who had lived in Naples; samples from the French school by Gaspard Dughet and Poussin; works by friends and models of his youth such as Girodet, de Desmarais, de Maynier, de Lethière, and Jacques Louis David. Add to this his own works in

The former Jesuit College (1682)

the neoclassical style. In 1835 the painter, art collector, art dealer, and curator preserved his own image for posterity in a self-portrait in the classical style. One is confronted by a man of about seventy years, gazing pensively at a distant point and standing before an imagined romantic landscape of forests and mountains. Dignity, a trace of melancholy, and ironic aloofness are all in this face with the prominent nose and the energetic chin; at least one gets an idea of the personality of the Museum's founder.

While Fabre was still alive, a further important donation was made by the Montpellier stock broker Antoine Valedau (1777–1836). The Museum owes to him the wonderful paintings by Northern French and Flemish masters which most felicitously complement its collection of French and Italian masters. Of the many works of this collection, suffice it to mention the "Allegory" by Peter

Paul Rubens, the dozen paintings by Teniers, the Dutchman Jan Steen, and the splendid pictures by Greuze.

A further major addition to the Museum came from the Montpellier artist and art patron Alfred Bruyas (1821–1877). As the son of a rich local banker, he first studied at the Art Institute and then lived in Italy for a time, where he met Alexandre Cabanel in Rome. From 1849 he was in Paris, where he began acquiring pictures for what would become a large collection of paintings, buying Diaz, Millet, Delacroix, and Tassaert. He made friends with Delacroix and particularly with Courbet, with whom he travelled to Montpellier in 1854. This stay in Montpellier is documented in the Museum by several outstanding works by Courbet, especially "The Seashore at Palavas" and "The Meeting." In 1868 Bruyas donated 91 paintings to the Museum; after his death it received 60 more and a great number of drawings. Bruyas collected exclusively contemporary artists, who can be subdivided into three schools: the classicists (Cabanel and Bénonville), the romantics (Delacroix), and the realists (Courbet and Tassaert). However, Bruyas had no nose for future greatness. Thus he took no notice of Cézanne or his fellow citizen Frédéric Bazille.

It remains to mention the donations made during the 18th and 19th centuries by the families of the artists Alexandre Cabanal and Frédéric Bazille. Thanks to the generosity of the Bazille family, the Museum owns the most important collection of works by this precursor of impressionism, friend of Renoir, Sisley, and Monet. What might not have become of this brilliant son of the city, if he hadn't laid down his life at age 29 on a battlefield of the Franco-Prussian War?

In spite of the limited funds of a university city without a significant industrial zone, the skilled leadership of the Museum's curators has enabled it to pursue a wise acquisition policy in this century, so that works by Utrillo, Othon Friez, André Lhote, Robert Delaunay, etc. could be purchased. The visitor will surely not fail to notice that more recent styles in art history, such as the Fauvists, cubism, surrealism, and the *avant-garde*, are poorly represented. Perhaps cultural decentralization and the expansion of technological industry will allow for providing current trends in art the space they deserve. At any rate, this is one of the most beautiful provincial museums in France and eloquent testimony of the art appreciation of the bourgeoisie, mirroring a century and a half of cultural life in the city.

"The Poetry of Love in Passion and Melancholy." Triptych of the sculptor Antoine Injalbert (Boulevard Bonne Nouvelle)

In the Municipal Library

The Museum Atger

How many cultivated and interested citizens of Montpellier have never laid eyes on the unique collection of drawings and sketches housed in the Faculty of Medicine and bearing the name of its donor, Atger?

Here, too, we notice a tendency characteristic of this city long dominated by the bourgeoisie and an office-holding elite, a tendency to handle wealth and art treasures discreetly, not to flaunt them. But what is so special about this rich, splendid collection of drawings owned by the revered old Faculty of Medicine, a collection which in its one-hundred-and-fifty-year history has only once been exhibited in another city, at the "Cabinet des Dessins du Musée du Louvre" (October 1974 to January 1975)?

Xavier Atger was born in Montpellier in 1758, the son of a merchant. He studied medicine and philosophy in his native city and showed an early interest in all the important intellectual tendencies of the time; he was particularly impressed by Lavater's studies of physiognomy. Without ample means or a post, he moved to Paris in 1802, remaining there until 1823 and only returning to Montpellier on his retirement. In Paris he devoted his free time to adding to the collection of drawings, sketches, and engravings he had begun as a knowledgeable art lover. He devoted particular attention to the artists of the Midi, giving priority to "movement in the drawings." In keeping with the spirit of the times, all of these artists had been to Rome, but they had definitely preserved their own stylistic autonomy, characteristic of the Midi. Thus, in Atger's collection we find Bourdon from Montpellier and La Fage from Albi; the great sculptor Puget, who preferred his native Provence to Paris, where he felt unappreciated; Antoine Rivalz and Jean III of Troy, both founders and directors of art academies in their native provinces of Toulouse and Montpellier; the masterly, sensitive Subleyras, who stayed in Rome; Natoire, Director of the "School of Rome;" the important portrait painters Rigaud and Fragonard, in whose work the sensibility, passion, and verve of their age attain a harmonious symbiosis. With the instinct of a connoisseur he enriched his collection by including nearly all the great names of the French 17th and 18th centuries. Bouchardon, Coypel, Philippe of Champaigne, Huet, Oudry, Simon Vouet . . . The Italian school is also prominently represented with works by Caravaggio, Parmigianino, Cambiaso, Palmieri, etc. There are also some surprises from the Flemish, Dutch, and German schools: Breughel, Van Dyck, Spranger, Ridinger, and particularly a masterly sketch by Peter Paul Rubens, "Susanna in the Bath."

Xavier Atger gave these drawings, collected over many years, as a donation to the Faculty of Medicine of his native city between 1813 and 1833. The donation was meant not just as a decoration for the voluminous library; he wanted his drawings to be "a source of recreation for the students, to sharpen their faculties for observing nature and to preserve the memory of the meridional artists who have contributed to the history of art during their lifetime."

*A painting by the Nîmes artist
Charles Natoire (1700–1777) in the
Museum Atger*

Xavier Atger lived to have the personal satisfaction of seeing his collection housed in the Faculty of Medicine he so dearly loved. And even today, after several restorations and an evacuation during the German occupation in World War II, it is on exhibit in St. Benedict College, founded by Pope Urban V, the seat of the Faculty of Medicine. The art lover who takes the trouble to descend to the former library of the Bishop (in the Faculty building), where the collection has found a worthy setting, will be rewarded by a very special kind of experience.

During the auspicious administration of Dean Giraud, the artworks underwent restoration in the years 1954 to 1964 and were then placed in their present cunningly-designed display cases. Only once has this rare collection been on display outside Montpellier: from October 1974 to January 1975, when it was exhibited at the "Cabinet des Dessins" in the Louvre.

*Next double spread:
The stand of the Four Seasons
greengrocer (rue de l'Herberie)*

Montpellier's Cuisine

Taking a morning stroll through the cool, narrow streets of the medieval section called the "Ancien Courrier" – or in the vicinity of the Cathedral or the Church of St. Anne – to enjoy the colourful play of light of the slanting rays of sunlight and the hard lines separating light and shadow on centuries-old walls one will, will here and there, encounter a pleasantly pungent aroma deriving its character from the white garlic bulb and suggestive of a cuisine owing its richness to the Mediterranean, the herb-rich Garrigue, and the endless vineyards. Arriving at the bustling market galleries, where one can feel the pulse of life in the Midi, where its gay chatter and irrepressible mobility – its sensuality, in a word – come to the fore, where what precious harvests the sea and mountains nearby can provide are displayed in all hues and forms, the synaesthetic morning sensations of the wanderer reach a climax. With the anticipative palate of the gourmet, he will wonder what particular joys of the table this city, which was always open to trade with the Occident, the Orient, and the Levant, may have to offer.

Let's admit at the outset that one can't speak of a characteristic Montpellieran cuisine the way we are accustomed, say, to referring to Lyon's. There are a few gastronomic specialties, to be sure, which one associates with Montpellier, such as *oreillettes de Montpellier,* a pancake fried in olive oil which was originally rolled out on the knee – like the South German *fastnacht* cakes – and "Montpellier snails", stewed in an aromatic sauce of olive oil, raw lean bacon, almonds, anchovies, and garlic. But there are no main courses bearing the name of the city. Its cuisine is rather an expression of the ability to take up influences from abroad and assimilate them.

What *joie de vivre,* what pristine sense for making the most of the sometimes modest fruits of the Mediterranean countryside the visitor discovers when observing the Montpellierans at table! They don't just sit down to table, they celebrate their cuisine like a mass, for they have the three holy ingredients of Christianity at their disposal: the oil of the olive tree, the good red wine from the plains and slopes of the Hérault, and the day's crisp, fresh bread. And the coast has everything that sea and lagoons have to offer in fish and shellfish.

Oysters and mussels come for the most part from the Etang de Thau, a nearby lagoon. A special event in the mild evenings of early summer is the *brazucade* with the mussels of Bouzigues. The mussels are cleaned of seaweed and grilled in their shells on a big grill preheated with vine branches. When they open over the lively fire, a few drops of a sauce made of tomatoes, garlic, onions, parsley, diced raw ham, and dry white wine are trickled onto them. With a dry white wine from the area such as "Picpoul de Pinet" or a "Clairette" – which must of course be served chilled – these mussels are delicious. Not only in the good restaurants of the city, but in many a private kitchen, too, the "sea wolf" is a specialty. It is one of the best Mediterranean fishes, and it is usually grilled with

Everybody knows her:
the garlic and lemon vender

93

a hollowroot stuffing. Freshly caught sardines, carefully scaled and cleaned and grilled over vine wood, are among the simple delicacies of the area and are often the main attraction at festivities in gardens and parks in the early summer, when the mild evenings filled with the scents of the sea and the Garrigue lure people out into the open.

Another specialty, which is grilled in the open over vine wood, is the delicious pork sausage one can buy by the yard at the butcher's. It is rolled up like a snail, spiced with herbs from the Garrigue, particularly thyme, and then carefully roasted over the coals. This delicacy tastes best when the sausage is about 24 hours old and is pierced several times with a fork to let off the fat. In the autumn during the wine harvest, on the last day of the tedious work, this specialty is grilled in the fields, and the enticing, typical grill smell of the vine wood is then mixed with the sweetly putrid aroma of the fermenting mash.

In the country around Montpellier, as in the shoreline areas of the Languedoc and Roussillon in general, fish dishes are frequently cooked in a very tasty sauce, which, probably due to its rusty-red colour, was given the name "sauce américaine" or sometimes "sauce armoricaine." The recipe won't be given here – it can easily found in local cookbooks. Suffice it to remark that its complicated preparation involves a good peanut oil, a few crevettes, shrimps, onions, challots, plenty of garlic, parsley, celery, laurel, tomato paste etc. In this wonderful sauce, shellfish such as prawns, lobsters, squids, etc. are boiled for 10 to 15 minutes. This dish is best served with a chilled *rosé* from St. Cristol or St. Saturnin.

Of course, the Garrigue asserts itself with several outstanding dishes on the Montpellierans' menu. Take, for example, rabbit stewed in local dry white wine with the three main spices of the area: sage, savoury, and thyme, which is best served with a fruity *rosé* from the "Coteaux du Languedoc." Or take quail flamed with armagnac, cognac, or "Fine de Languedoc" on a *canapé* (a slice of bread roasted in butter); or a leg of mutton or lamb larded with garlic, from local animals, whose meat is particularly tasty thanks to the rich, good grasses of the Garrigue or the plateau.

And finally, the highlands, the "Haut Pays," should not be forgotten: the rocky, wind-exposed elevated areas of the Cevennes and Larzac with their deep crevasses and clear waters and rivers. From there come the river crabs cooked in a strong sauce, the fresh trout that can be served as "trout with almonds," "trout with sorrel," or "trout in cream sauce."

But in the Languedoc or Montpellier, the same is true as elsewhere: what would a meal be without cheese? Here cheese enjoys the good reputation of making one immune to all illnesses. Roquefort can be bought from the local cheese mongers in several varieties coming fresh from the cellar vaults of the Larzac. With it, many interesting dishes can be prepared or improved upon, such as the tender *feuilletés au Roquefort* or *entrecôte au Roquefort*.

The variety of goat's cheese is also wide, ranging from creamy to hard as a rock. What a delicacy to take fresh, creamy goat's cheese and cover it with a layer of herbs from the Garrigue and roast it for 10 to 15 minutes in the oven!

*Market in the morning
on Place Castellane*

*"The old oven", one of many nice
restaurants, predominantly frequented
by students*

The archaic pleasures of the palate, enjoyed in a happy group under the bright sky of the Midi: one is in harmony with this Occitanian soil, its culture, and its people when the cornucopia of the fruits of the sea, the Garrigue, the plateaus, and the vineyards is emptied onto the table. Delight in the unadulterated, as the wise Joseph Delteil puts it in his "Cuisine of the Paleolithic:"

"... Take a thick slice of stale bread, both crust and inside. Rub garlic into it devotedly as long as possible. Pour oil and vinegar the length and breadth of it: make a veritable road map of it. The trick is that both should mix well, that the oil penetrates the whole mass ... go ahead and take bite ... it's like in earthly paradise."

Try it, with a wine of your choice!

Buildings on the Place de la Comédie, with the copper roofs typical of the end of the 19th century

The modernized Place de la Comédie (1986)

Boulevard Henri IV

*The Grand'rue Jean Moulin, one of the
main arteries since the Middle Ages*

The smile of Montpellier. Sculptures
in the courtyard of the Hôtel d'Allut (c. 1740)

The Palace of Flaugergues.
Stairway in the style of the 17th century

The Palace of Flaugergues,
built about 1700

The Palace of La Piscine, built about 1770

The Palace of Mosson (1723): monumental fountain decorated with clam shells

The Palace of Mogère, built about 1715

*Hôtel de Mirman with its
staircase (17th century)*

*The hôtel des Trésoriers-de-France, also
called Lunaret, built at the spot of Jacques
Cœur's former palais (17th century)
on the street of the same name*

Place St.-Ravy: a Gothic bay window in the façade of a medieval hôtel

Wrought-iron bannister of the grand staircase of the Hôtel des Trésoriers-de-France

Entryway and façade of the
Hôtel des Trésoriers-de-la-Bourse

Doorknockers, witnesses of a lost art

The Hôtel des Trésoriers-de-la-Bourse or Hôtel Bonnier-de-la-Mosson (rue Trésoriers-de-la-Bourse)

Passageway of rue Voltaire leading under the "Arc-de-Coulondres" to rue Vallat

*Roofscape in the
historic centre*

111

Antigone

The visitor flying in from the North will be surprised to notice a monumental building project just a few hundred yards from the heraldic-shield-shaped historic centre. Just ten years ago, this was a barren, barracks-strewn military complex on the far side of the railroad tracks; now it is one of the most remarkable and controversial urban development projects in Europe. It all began with the decision by the Socialist city government under Mayor Georges Frêche to create a new, humane way of living together in deliberate contrast to the Polygone business centre initiated in the sixties by his predecessor, François Delmas. The famous but also controversial neoclassicist Ricardo Bofill was hired as chief architect. The powerful theatre backdrop in a style reminiscent of antiquity was completed in less than a decade, thanks to a new, complicated poured-concrete technique.

Coming from the Polygone via the connecting Echelles de la Ville, which the architect intended to symbolize a transition from history to the present, one first arrives at the theatre backdrop of the Square of the Golden Section (Place du Nombre d'Or), glistening in a radiant yellowish ochre. The name alone, in signaling harmonious proportions, is indicative of what the architect had in mind. And indeed, the ratios of the ground plan, pilasters, and sculptures are based on the Golden Section: a return to antiquity, joy in symmetry and axes, the symbolism of perspectives: the mutual intersecting of squares and circles. Feeling tiny and somewhat intimidated, the viewer stands before this sweeping gesture. His gaze involuntarily moves up the respect-inspiring façade to where the radiant blue Mediterranean sky arches over the pergola gables. From the centre of the square, the scene, in which the viewer feels quite insignificant, shifts to the power-radiating central axis. In this dream of a postmodernist ideal city realized in concrete, nothing has been left to chance. Names such as Thousand-year Square, Thessaly Square, Hadrian's Villa, Athena, Thebes, and Les Espaces d'Abraxas are indicative of the project's foundations in the origins of European architectural and cultural tradition.

Through archways which seem like theatre props, one can see all the way to the fountains on the Lez. Behind them, on the far bank, is a large modern building, the seat of the regional government. In a sweeping gesture, the huge semicircle of the Port Juvenal building opens like an amphitheatre on the revamped harbour facilities of the river, thus stressing Montpellier's original ties with the sea.

Thus, the municipal government has built an impressive satellite city at the end of the century, with 2,200 real-estate units: council flats, owner-occupied flats, shops, and offices. On this 60-acre plot, just a couple of stone's throws from the historic centre, a dwelling model worth talking about has been built in answer to the frigidity and bleakness of so many dormitory suburbs. Communal infrastructure such as schools, children's facilities, churches, a house of labour and trade unions, and recreational facilities are included; as are shops, bars, restaurants, and the seat of the Regional Government of Languedoc-Roussillon.

The future will show whether this social utopia, now become a monument, can be filled with the contemplative and joyful activity customary of the little streets around the Place de la Comédie. At any rate, Montpellier has one more architectural sight which attracts prominent visitors from throughout the world and is eloquent testimony of the imagination and ambitious plans of the municipal government.

*Antigone, the new section of the city designed
by Ricardo Bofill. The Places
du Nombre d'Or and du Millénaire*

Taking the Road to Modernism

A glance at the Montpellier of the early sixties from today's perspective reveals the astonishing metamorphosis the city has undergone in a period of just three decades. The self-sufficient, quiet university city of that time, with a population of not quite 100,000, has turned into a still growing, youthful regional capital vibrating with life. University affairs, then conducted in the historic centre, are now carried out in courses and research at three universities with 50,000 students, living and working for the most part in campuses on the outskirts. The city's appearance then, with its silhouette stemming from the end of the 19th century, with its historic centre unchanged in its architectural substance, has developed into an area of concentration whose satellite cities spread out over the countryside like the arms of a polyp. What are the reasons, which factors are responsible for Montpellier's rapid ascension to a large city, to an international meeting place of culture, research, and high technology of wide repute? The magical attraction of the Languedoc's sun belt must have been accompanied by other events for a chain reaction of growth processes to be unleashed at the suitable moment in history.

Even at the threshhold of the new era, in 1958/60, the first tendencies of a population increase become noticeable. The continual growth of the University and other institutions of higher learning, the resulting increase in the number of students, the expansion of the service industries, and the influx of immigrant workers from the Maghreb are given as reasons. In the autumn of 1961 the City Council votes to build the first satellite city, La Paillade, to the Northwest, some four miles from the city's centre. It is designed to house 40,000 people. From this time on, the stations on Montpellier's way to becoming one of the leading cities of the French Mediterranean region follow in rapid succession. In 1962 the city and its environs have to absorb the flow of "black-feet" refugees, the Algerian French, and the "Harkis," the Algerian colonial militia (25,000 in all), who come to settle in Montpellier and the surrounding region after Algeria's declaration of independence. This was a great challenge to the municipal authorities at the time, and one can understand why from this time on a veritable growth ideology pervades official pronouncements. Between 1962 and 1968, Montpellier grows by another 42,000 inhabitants, thus setting a French record for growth, which it will keep for many years.

Within the scope of a new regionalization policy, the central government had already decided at the beginning of the sixties to make Montpellier the capital of the region of Languedoc-Roussillon. This became reality in 1964. This new function brought a number of positive state-subsidized supportive measures to the city, such as the accelerated expansion of the administrative bureaucracy and transportation systems. Up to this time, the university clinics, private hospitals, and the various university facilities were the large entities in the city's economic life. This situation underwent a fundamental change, with far-reaching effects on the economic structure of the region, with the establishment

Window by Renée Rauzy in the Church of Don Bosco (Antigone)

The commercial centre Le Triangle

of an IBM computer-manufacturing plant in 1964/65. Within a very short time, the plant, located in the city's La Pompignane section, was employing a staff of 2,000 skilled workers, highly qualified specialists, and engineers. The company initiated the establishment of a network of about 30 suppliers in the city and environs, some of them as far away as Alès and Ganges. This was designed to stimulate the region's economy further, but also made it dependent on company policy. The establishment of a world-wide company in the field of high technology was not only of vital importance for the employment situation and export capacity of greater Montpellier, but also for the introduction of a modern conception of economic efficiency and technological advancement. Today, the Montpellier IBM plant is one of the four manufacturing facilities IBM has in France. It is one of the plants in the world which manufactures all of the top computers of the 3090 series, the models 150 to 600, and the thermal control modules (T.C.M.), the most important component of the central processing unit; the productivity of its employees is remarkably high. IBM's dominant role in the city's and region's economy is reflected in the import-export percentages of the region of Languedoc-Roussillon: in 1987, the plant accounted for 45.1 % of the exports and 19.4 % of imports. IBM's close relations with the entire scientific and economic complex of the "technopolis" will be the subject of a later chapter.

At that time the municipal government also tried to attract the pharmaceutical industry to Montpellier, where they could avail themselves of the existing infrastructure of the pharmaceutical and medical faculties, the National School of Chemistry, and the National Institute of Health and Medical Research. And indeed, a few such companies, of which Clin Midy is the most significant, established themselves on the city's northern periphery.

In this period of feverish construction activity in the public and private sectors, the spacious university campus was also begun on the city's periphery, featuring many student dwelling complexes surrounded by large parks. The then Faculty of Natural Sciences and now University of Montpellier II (University of Sciences and Technology of the Languedoc – U.S.T.L.) and the then Faculty of the Humanities and now University of Montpellier III – Paul Valéry stretch out on both sides of the main highway towards Mende on an area the size of the city's historic centre. The problems of space were solved for the moment, but this transposition of a major portion of university activity brought on a change in the social structure of the city's central sections – many of the cultural events in the spirit of current trends took place in the "Amphithéâtres" at Paul Valéry University. It was the time when many of the inhabitants of the historic centre made pilgrimages to the campus of Paul Valéry University to see films at the Jean Vigo Film Club and take part in the lively discussions afterwards, spiritedly chaired by Pierre Pitiot and Henri Talvet, or to see theatre productions by Jacques Bioulès. In the city, the late but unforgotten André Croq succeeded, in his cosmopolitan, tolerant way, in turning the small cultural centre of the Languedoc into a centre of intellectual debate and exciting cultural confrontation. One still fondly remembers the

*Hôtel St.-Côme, formerly the dissection
amphitheatre of the surgeon Lapeyronie, built
by Jean-Antoine Giral in 1752–1757.
Today it is the seat of the Chamber of Industry
and Commerce*

The Esplanade

atmosphere of anticipation in the narrow, overcrowded lobby when writers, painters, and actors crowded around the jovial host at exhibition openings or theatre performances.

In these years, partnerships with other cities were also established; the townspeople widely applauded them as a good way to international understanding. The first partner cities were Barcelona, Heidelberg, and Louisville.

The rapid population growth and the newly acquired role of centre of regional government and administration furthered the expansion of administrative facilities and the growth and modernization of business and trade. The large construction projects of the financial administration, the Houses of Agriculture and of National Insurance were carried out. The largest construction project of those years was realized just 1,000 ft. from the Place de la Comédie on a vacant plot on the far side of the railroad tracks: the business and administrative centre called Polygone. A modern ensemble of several stories features large department stores such as Galeries Lafayette, Inno, C & A, and the FNAC; cinemas, snackbars, and banks. Close by the mirrored front is the new Town Hall in all its cool efficiency; from its roof terrace, the aldermen have a commanding panorama of the historic centre, the Citadel, and the lagoons. In this overheated growth of a city which had been catapulted from a hundred-years' sleep into a new orbit, the municipal government, with its traditional ties to liberalism, found itself faced with large-scale real-estate speculation and construction activity overflowing in all directions. Villa developments and multiple-dwelling blocks sprang up where a short time before roads bordered by stone walls had trailed off into the vineyards and hilly landscape of the Garrigue.

The birth of Greater Montpellier occurred while Mayor François Delmas, who had taken up the management of the city's affairs in 1959, was in office. He was the son of a professor at the Faculty of Medicine and a lawyer by profession. He had an impressive gift for speaking, was a Conservative with a penchant for Europe and the advocate of a distinct economic liberalism of the American variety. He headed the city government for three terms. He skillfully managed to remain above the political squabbles and tensions of his own coalition without taking a definite party stance. However, in his third term, a clear discrepancy between demographic and economic growth became apparent: the political significance of the city on the one hand was contrasted by an insufficient, outmoded cultural programme on the other.

On the Way to "Heliopolis"

Montpellier's exemplary development into an attractive regional capital whose reputation is spreading more and more throughout Europe would have been inconceivable to this degree without the expert central and regional planning of tourism. The first step in this direction was the establishment in 1955 of the Interdepartmental Association for Combatting Mosquitoes in the Departments of Hérault, Gard, and Bouches-du-Rhône. Then, under President De Gaulle,

Le Peyrou und the Church
of Saint Anne by night

the Interdepartmental Mission for Coastal Administration was established to modernize the coastal area of Languedoc-Roussillon. It initiated a gigantic building and investment programme to provide access to over 100 miles of shoreline from the mouth of the Rhône to the Pyrenees. Within 20 years, five new holiday developments, some of them with futuristic architecture such as Grande Motte, were built, along with twelve yacht harbours, open-air zoos, and sports facilities. Besides Grande Motte, the newly built or expanded beach towns of Port Camargue, Carnon, Palavas, and Cap d'Agde with their port facilities are also in Montpellier's direct sphere of influence. The building industry, banks, and trade – the entire business community, in short – underwent tremendous expansion by this activation of tourism which ultimately attracted five to six million tourists into the area per year. In this way, Montpellier and its environs were inflated to a region of a million people during the summer-holiday season, and the large shopping malls which have been built on the periphery, the ambitious cultural programme developed in recent years, and the historic centre made attractive by restoration have drawn many international summer guests into the area.

But it isn't just the general trend that decides on the continuation of a city's history; leading personalities are also always needed to orchestrate them. A turning point in the life of the city came in the spring of 1977 with the election of the Socialist Georges Frêche as Mayor of a grand leftist coalition. This was an all the more radical turn of events as Montpellier had been governed by a centre-right coalition for decades. This young energetic law professor at the University of Montpellier, an economist and historian, had already earned a name for himself as a deputy to the National Assembly. With him a new era in the history of the city has been initiated, characterized by an unmistakable style of its own, *le style Frêche*. On coming to power, he immediately set a publicly funded intervention policy in motion to provide the infrastructure lacking in a city which had undergone such hectic growth. In keeping with this, the cornerstone for the dominant urban project of the end of the millenium was already laid in 1979: the satellite city Antigone, designed by Bofill. Already at that time, Frêche's idea and that of his town planning adviser, the geography professor Dugrand, had crystallized: to extend the city in a further construction stage in the direction of the coast. In the meantime, the die has been cast: with Port Marianne, a second, even larger satellite city will be built next to Antigone; its planned harbour facilities will testify to Montpellier's historic connection to the *Mare Nostrum*. The new local government policies also included working out a new general transportation plan giving priority to public transportation and including spacious pedestrian zones.

"The stairways to the city" (Antigone)

Contemporary architecture (rue Doria)

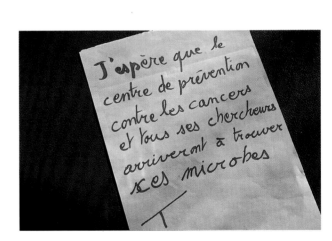

The Cancer Research Institute in the technology park "Eurománagement"

Entrance to Corum, the congressional palace with an opera theatre. An impressive block of granite and marble, designed by the architect Claude Vasconi

125

*On the grounds of Agropolis:
Agronomers in a blossoming cotton
field in . . . Montpellier!
(Domaine de Lavalette)*

Montpellier – the Beating Heart of the Languedoc

In Montpellier's City Council, not only various factions of the French Left are represented today; the last elections also showed an opening towards the centre and an increase of representatives without party affiliation. Key portfolios such as culture, architecture, urban affairs, health, and technology went to professors at the universities – Georges Frêche has succeeded in getting the universities to participate in municipal affairs. The decision of the City Council which would have the most lasting effect regarded the expansion of cultural life. Soon after gaining power in 1977, a graduated plan to this effect was passed. The goal was to make Montpellier the dominant cultural centre of the Languedoc, capable of also stimulating the surrounding region, which centuries of centralization policies had drained of all culture. This goal of giving the university city and regional capital a cultural and economic accent in the region gave rise to the handy slogan, "Montpellier, the Beating Heart of the Languedoc." But by activating social and cultural life, the groundwork was to be laid in particular for attracting the management of large technological companies to settle here. The funds invested in this policy were enormous for a city the size of Montpellier. During Frêche's first term, the expenditures for culture rose from 4 % to 12 % of the total budget. A municipal orchestra, a

Seat of the Regional Government,
completed in 1989 (architect Ricardo Bofill)

The Palace "Château d'O"
built about 1750

regional ballet ensemble (Centre Chorégraphique Régional), and a photography gallery were founded, and the Museum and Municipal Library expanded. The appointment of Jérome Savary as Manager and Artistic Director of the newly established Centre dramatique du Languedoc-Roussillon was not only a great boon to stimulating the cultural scene in the region, but also an important step for Montpellier on the way to becoming a cultural city of European stature. It was a time in which not only Savary's productions made their way to Paris and many European capitals, but the city's innate cultural energies were given the chance to develop. Initiatives encouraged painters, writers, and musicians to take part in enriching social and cultural life. The cultural tradition of the Languedoc, which hitherto had been cultivated solely by the pertinent department at the University, was opened to the broader public with city and regional support and reached new heights. In individual sections of the city the first "Maisons pour tous" were established, of which there are no less than 13 today. In a city with a tradition of peaceful coexistence of Jews, Arabs, and Christians; with the oldest medical school, which experienced such a felicitous development thanks to the tolerant cooperation of scholars of these three faiths; but whose history was also marred by centuries of bloody conflict between Protestants and Catholics, it should be applauded that the municipal authorities have succeeded in getting all of these different cultural communities involved in the city's cultural life.

Building of the Departmental Council and the Château Alco (1744)

The Cultural Scene

In the space of ten years, Montpellier has become an art and cultural city of European standing. Beginning with the extant cultural institutions and the cultural tradition of a university city which had developed over the centuries and which had already established a conservatory of music, the Museum Fabre, and an Art Institute within its walls, and whose 19th-century opera house provided a splendid ambience for concerts and opera, new centres of cultural encounter and international festivals were founded. Surely the initiators aimed not only to raise the quality of cultural life to new heights, but also to ensure that a democratization of cultural activities is attained in a city growing steadily younger.

Under the direction of its General Manager, Henri Maier, the Opera has a sophisticated and in part unconventional repertoire, for which outstanding soloists are brought in (it has no permanent ensemble). Soon this opera house furnished in the magnificent style of the last century will have a younger cohort: the Corum congressional palace will have a "Berlioz Hall" with a capacity of 2,200 people. On the occasion of the old house's centennial in 1988, not only was Meyerbeer's opera "Les Huguenots" performed, with which it had been opened, but a cooperation contract was also agreed upon with several European opera houses to exchange productions. As part of the celebrations of the bicentennial of the French Revolution, the opera dealing with the Revolution by the contemporary composer Dussapin, "Romeo et Juliette," was premiered in 1989 and then went on a tour of French and other European opera houses. But what would the most beautiful opera house be without a permanent orchestra, which the city lacked for many years? The founding of the Philharmonic Orchestra of Montpellier Languedoc-Roussillon, with Cyril Diedrich as permanent conductor, goes back to 1978/79. In recent years this orchestra has acquired a good reputation beyond the confines of the Languedoc. With the Centre Choréographique National, which the choreographer Dominique Baguet was appointed to organize, Montpellier has acquired an international reputation as a stage of contemporary ballet. In a remodelled former wine cellar – part of the recreation, culture, and representation centre called Grammont – the Théâtre des Treize Vents, directed by Jacques Nichet, is located. This theatre director has not only succeeded in bringing the theatre public to an unaccustomed place on the city's edge to see his remarkable productions of modern and classical authors, he has also put on productions with his troupe in Paris and other French cities. Close by this theatre, the city built the Zenith concert hall, which looks like a futuristic circus tent, seats 6,600 people, and has a technical apparatus of the highest order. It is here that world-famous stars of show business perform for a predominantly young audience. It can also happen that 50,000 young people congregate under the summer stars of the Midi in the "Rock Stadium," i. e., the Espace Richter, as was the case when Bruce Springsteen came here.

A second-hand bookshop on rue de l'Université

133

Production of "Frankenstein"
after the novel by Mary Shelley
at the "Printemps des Comédiens"
(Château d'O)

In the same decade, Montpellier has undergone an astonishing development into a multi-faceted festival city. In July, the International Music Festival of Radio France and Montpellier, directed by René Koering, attracts a cultivated international public to the city. The direct transmissions broadcast to other European countries bear witness to the broad range of events featuring opera productions, classical and jazz concerts, and workshop discussions. In the ten years they have existed, the Journées Internationales de la Photographie et de l'Audiovisuel, which are held in May, have become a fixture in the cultural life of the city and the region. Add to this the Festival International Montpellier Danse, organized by Jean-Paul Montanari, which every June invites renowned dance theatres to give open-air performances in the festive setting of the Cour Jacques Cœur in the heart of the city's historic centre.

The visitor desiring to acquaint himself with the city's way of life will soon notice the important role the medium film plays in Montpellier. There are not only a sizable number of cinemas, but also several active student film clubs showing Spanish, Anglo-American, German, and Italian films. Only recently,

*A famous Montpellieran,
the actor Galabru with François Sayad*

In the studio of the painter Gérard Calvet

this infrastructure has brought forth the Rencontres avec le Cinéma Méditerranéen and also festivals of Jewish, Israeli, and Chinese films. The centre of gravity of these encounters with the international film world is the fine municipal film theatre Rabelais on the Esplanade close to the Museum Fabre.

The opening of the city's cultural life to the world at large is underscored by its city partnerships with Barcelona, Heidelberg, Louisville, Tiberia (Israel), and Chengdu (China). These often involve lively cultural exchanges.

With the "Maisons pour tous," meeting places open to everyone were established, with the aim of providing informal access to culture and education. Municipal art galleries such as the Artothèque, the Galerie St. Ravy, the Médiathèque Gutenberg, and the photography gallery in the Corum complement the richly faceted image of a Mediterranean city of culture which looks on its responsibility to provide culture as a service to the citizens.

The characterization of Montpellier as a youthful city with a strong recreational component would be incomplete if sports went unmentioned as an exciting element of the city's life; its development in such a broad context would not be possible without the support of public sponsors. There are some 600 athletic clubs in the city; three of them, in basketball, volleyball, and football (soccer), wear the city's blue colour in the 1st division and at international matches. The Mosson Stadium of Montpellier's La Paillade football club was expanded and modernized in recent years, so that it has already found use for international matches (France vs. West Germany). The "Nicollin Club," as it is called after its popular and ebullient president, has made it into France's 1st Division, a respectable feat, and was in the UEFA Cup tournament two years ago.

From Technopolis to Eurocité?

For several years Montpellier has been diligently pursuing its further development into a "Technopolis." A huge media campaign was launched to advertise the city's intention of participating in the third industrial revolution, that of information science and electronics, after having missed the boat on the first two in the past. These efforts are guided by the idea that modern urban planning and the combined effects of research and teaching, of culture and sports are the foundations for economic development. Thus, for a city to reach the rank of a technopolis, there must be a global vision. This requires a strategy coordinating municipal authorities with the universities and their research facilities with companies in the high-tech sector. The initial position for this campaign to turn Montpellier into a technopolis was as good as one could wish. With its three universities and 50,000 students, six national institutions at the "Grande Ecole" level, several CNRS's (Centre Nationale de Recherche Scientifique), employing 350 researchers, the city has an intricate network of scientific and technological potential to offer. One quarter of Montpellier's population is in the academic sector. Besides, Montpellier already had a traditional reputation in two fields of science: medical and agricultural research.

In a surprisingly short period, the ambitious plan of a five-pole technological capital in Southern Europe was realized, as shown by building projects extending throughout the entire area of the greater city.

The development of electronic components in a sterile room (University of Science and Technology – Montpellier II)

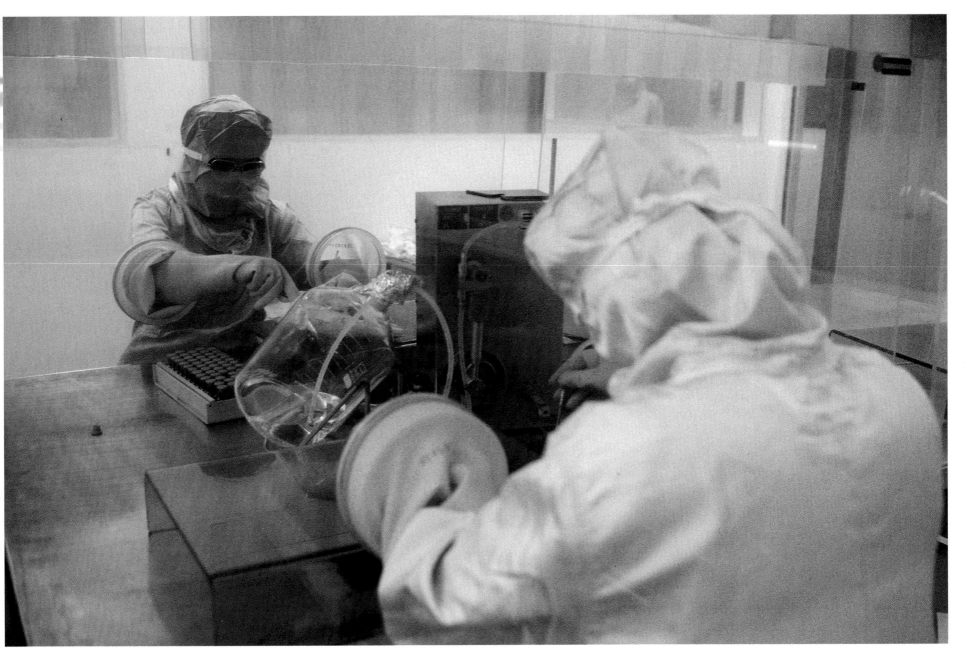

The Parc Euromédecine is located on a 370-acre plot in the city's northwest area. Needless to say, medical and pharmaceutical research found good starting conditions in the already extant laboratories and research units of the Faculty of Medicine, with its great tradition; the university hospitals of St. Eloi, Saint Charles, Gui-de-Chauliac, and Lapeyronie; and the Faculty of Pharmacy, thus making Montpellier attractive for companies in the biomedical and pharmaceutical sectors. Some 100 companies, with 3,500 employees, have taken up quarters in this park, where they are in close proximity to the C.N.R.S., the I.N.S.E.R.M. (National Institute of Health and Medical Research), and the laboratories of the university hospitals. If an international company such as Sanofi is engaged in research here, this means that it has the conglomerate ELF Aquitaine behind it; it has a highly qualified staff of 650 people. In 1985 the international trade fair called Euromédecine was opened, another idea of Georges Frêche's. This annual event has meanwhile become the largest European fair in the field of medicine, with the goal of making the results of medical research accessible to a broader public.

Agronomy can build on a solid traditional foundation in Montpellier, and in the field of tropical agronomy, it enjoys global fame. Already in 1870/72 the Ecole Nationale d'Agriculture was founded. Nonetheless, outsiders will

hardly suspect the role this satellite research city plays in the national framework, not to mention that of development aid and North-South cooperation. Who could guess that in this science park, Montpellier has in a way become the world banana capital? In the laboratories of the IRFA (Institute of Fruit and Tropical-fruit Research), new banana plants which are better adapted to their environment are being developed *in vitro* by gene manipulation. In many other fields, such as research on rice cultivation and the improvement of cotton production, the results of research conducted in Agropolis are of far-reaching significance for the developing countries. 1,800 researchers are working in 18 different instruction and research units dealing with the agro-industry, hydrotechnology, agrotechnology, forestry, farming-machine applications – particularly in the Mediterranean countries – plant-gene research, information science, and robot technology.

The final stage of this research complex will be the Agropolis Museum, planned for 1992. It is intended as a showcase of the agricultural research going on in Montpellier, to show the relationships between science, technology, and society in the agriculture of the Mediterranean countries.

As has already been pointed out, IBM established one of its most important plants for manufacturing its top range of computers in Montpellier in the

There are some 50,000 students in Montpellier

sixties. This leading company has in the meantime accumulated a sizable network of smaller companies in the fields of automation and artificial intelligence. Close cooperation between IBM and France's second-largest university computer centre, the C.N.U.S.C., is one result, particularly in the area of intensive digital computation.

Montpellier Languedoc-Roussillon Technopole has profited from the existence of these two large communications operations by founding an organization called Cap Alpha, which assists young companies in getting started in this innovative field. With the support of the European Community, this initiative has now become the European Centre for Enterprise and Innovation. Many of these smaller companies have found quarters in the Parc du Millénaire in the city's southeastern section. However, this conglomeration of monotonous block-style buildings sticking up along the freeway connection can hardly be called a model of innovative contemporary architecture.

After individual sections of the city had been provided with light-wave-conducting cables and a local television facility had been set up, an International Picture Centre and the Mediathèque Gutenberg were founded. In this complex of new means of communication the I.D.A.T.E. (Institute for the Develop-

In the professors' wardrobe at the University

ment of Audiovisual and Telecommunications in Europe), the national centre Arts et Métiers, and a journalists' training centre are also located.

At the southern entrance to the city, on the lawn in front of the satellite city Antigone, is the name Heliopolis, reminiscent of the world of antiquity. The city fathers, never at a loss for billboard names, use this one to suggest that the city is a sun temple: the creative city in Europe's South which, with its historic centre, its university life, its theatres, its museums, its newly designed parks, and green zones, its hundred fountains, the huge urban projects Antigone and Port Marianne, its scientific potential, but also the charm of the richly varied, lovely landscape surrounding it, attracts guests from throughout the world. Today, Montpellier is a city in which cultural tourism plays a significant role. With the Corum congressional centre by the architect Claude Vasconi the regional capital acquired an important instrument for the further development of congressional and business tourism adapted to today's requirements. The multifunctional Berlioz Hall has a capacity of 2,200 people and can be used for operas, congresses, and concerts. What a feat for the city of Montpellier, which had a population of 100,000 twenty years ago and is today, along with Paris, Nice, and Strasbourg, one of the four largest congressional cities in the country!

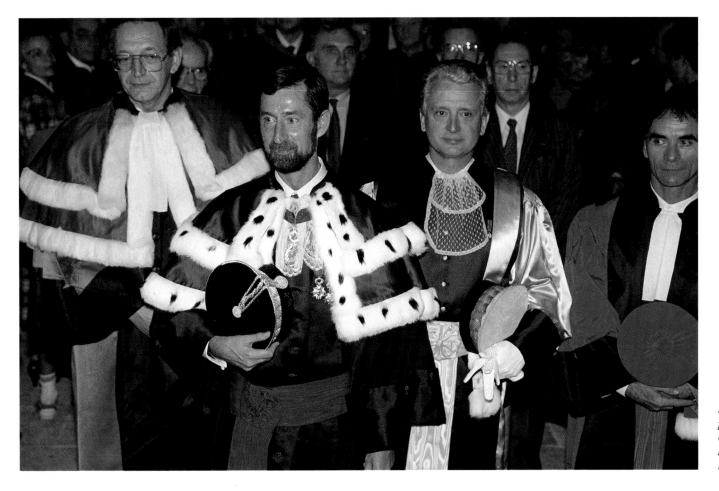

Solemn procession of the professors into the Cathedral of St. Peter on the 700th anniversary of the University in October, 1989

The Isle of Maguelone

"Have you, most gentle reader, ever become very distressed in your soul at how sad it is that the swirling wheel of time keeps on turning and that what was formerly at the top will soon be brought to the bottom?"

From "The Love Story of the Fair Maguelone and Count Peter of Provence," by Ludwig Tieck.

A stone's throw from the city gates, over the shimmering expanse of the lagoon, the wooded line of hills on the Isle of Maguelone can be seen. Windblown, gnarled pines guard the stone bulwark of faith, the awe-inspiring early-Romanesque Basilica of Maguelone. A pause in time, a respite from history. A place of peace and refuge, contemplation and prayer, where what has survived casts its spell over us: the mighty ruin of the Cathedral and the Cross.

This fortified church is what remains today as a powerful symbol of the two thousand years of history this island, rising up out of the lagoon landscape, has seen. Its settlement goes back to prehistoric times. Phoenicians and Etruscans had anchoring spots and trading posts here. The Roman settlement in the Provincia Narboniensis and a small bishop's seat from the middle of the 6th century were further stages of its development, and then, during the rule of the Moors, it became "Port-Sarrasin." After his victory over the Moors, Charles Martel destroyed it completely in 737, as it had been their base for attacking the mainland.

Under the priest Arnaud I, a Cathedral in the Lombardian style was begun in 1040; the island again became a bishop's seat and then a Papal fief. Bishop Jean de Montlaur completed the building in 1170 by joining the mighty nave to the transept built by his predecessor and furnishing the whole with fortifications. From here he founded schools and became the lord and patron of the young University of Montpellier. The growth of the town of Montpellier, the flourishing of its university in the age of humanism gave Bishop G. Pellicier cause to move the episcopal seat to Montpellier in 1536. From then on intellectual and ecclesiastical life focus on Montpellier, and the former scene of centuries of enriching confrontation and dramatic conflict between various Mediterranean cultures gradually recedes from memory.

The Lagoon of Maguelone

The Legend of the Fair Maguelone

In the solemn semi-darkness of one of the Cathedral's side-chapels, the Chapel of the Holy Sepulchre, the visitor notices a splendid marble sarcophagus richly decorated with a diamond pattern. According to legend, this is the final resting place of the fair Maguelone so often celebrated in poetry.

It is the wondrous tale of the love of Count Peter of Provence for the incredibly beautiful Maguelone, daughter of the King of Naples. Peter, who meets Maguelone at her father's court, gives his beloved three precious rings sewn into a little purse as a token of his affection. Peter abducts Maguelone from the royal court in Naples. As they are fleeing together, the rings are stolen by a bird of prey that flies away with them over the sea, finally dropping them on a lonely island. Peter gives chase to the bird, is swept out to sea in his little boat and taken captive by the Saracens. He spends many years as a slave at the Sultan's court. The unhappy Maguelone, who believes her beloved is lost forever, retires to Port-Sarrasin, later called the Isle of Maguelone, to care for the poor. There she builds a chapel dedicated to St. Peter.

One day the three lost rings turn up in the stomach of a freshly caught fish and Maguelone gives up all hope of ever finding her beloved again. One day a ship arriving from Alexandria brings a sick man to Port-Sarrasin. Maguelone takes care of him without realizing that this is her beloved, but then he tells her of the odyssey caused by his misfortunes and mentions Maguelone's name. A few days later, the happily reunited couple is married by the Bishop in the Cathedral of St. Pierre in Port-Sarrasin.

The legend of the love of the beautiful Princess of Naples, Maguelone, for Count Peter of Provence is first treated in the European literary tradition in a 12th-century French tale of chivalry by Bernard of Trivier. In the following centuries the subject became very popular. The numerous works based on this story include the French tale of chivalry, "Histoire de Pierre de Provence et de la belle Maguelone" (1453), and "Maguelone à son ami Pierre de Provence" by C. Marot (1517). The story regained popularity when the German author Ludwig Tieck included the "Wondrous Love Story of the Fair Maguelone and Count Peter of Provence" in his collection of romantic "Fairy Tales" of 1797. Tieck's "Romances of the Fair Maguelone" were set to music by Johannes Brahms (op. 33).

The House of the Free Professions on rue Alfred Nobel

Conclusion

At the close of the 20th century, Montpellier has realized its destiny of becoming a *eurocité,* i. e., a city of invention, research, and artistic creativity (*eurocité,* from the Greek *eurein* = to find, invent). It wants to play a part in the concert of the major regional capitals and is willing to share in changes wrought in recent years in the development of the Europe of tomorrow. The near future will show how it has fared with its plan in the rivalry with other leading cities of the Western Mediterranean, such as Barcelona, Toulouse, and Marseille, in what is increasingly becoming a Europe of regions. And yet, what astonishing progress has been made in the space of not quite three decades! In spite of the population explosion, in spite of the new building activity and the energetically promoted participation in the 3rd industrial revolution, the university city which owed its beginnings to the tolerant cooperation of Arabs, Christians, and Jews has preserved its identity. The exciting thing these days, for those actively involved and old natives, new citizens, and visitors alike, is the experience of witnessing a new birth, of just being there. As everyone knows, every beginning has its magic, giving life new energy and making our grief over the past more tolerable. In spite of the obvious tension between traditional living customs and the demands the age of information place on its citizens, the city seems to go on shaping its fate with equanimity.

It is in keeping with the character of a picture book of this kind that the description must be fragmentary. In the plan of the whole, some of the readers may miss this specific aspect or that event worth relating. Nonetheless, the authors feel that a mosaic of the city made from the pretty stones presented here would turn out to be accurate. But in no case should the reader feel inhibited in trying to discover the idiosyncrasies and beauty of the city for himself. Then he might run across the friendly merchant in his spacious shop from the good old days, who sits down to the piano for his customers and rips off a few bars of classical music and asks the perplexed customer – now listener – to guess the composer. If he guesses right, he gets 10 % off with his next purchase!

*Aigues-Mortes, a remarkable
example of medieval fortification*

Pharmacy of Monsieur Luidgi,
formerly in the Faubourg Figuerolles,
today in the Apothecaries' Museum

The research facilities of the SANOFI company
in Montpellier, which specializes in the
development of new drugs

A familiar sight to Montpellierans: boules players

Chronology

985	Donation of "Mont Pestelario" to Guilhem by the Count of Melgueil und his wife.
circa 1100	The first teachers of medicine appear on the scene.
1141	Rebellion of the Montpellierans against Guilhem VI.
1180	Charta of Guilhem VIII regarding the teaching of medicine.
1196	The first city walls are built: "Commune Clôture."
1204	Marriage of Marie of Montpellier with Pedro of Aragon: Charta of Montpellier.
1213–1276	Jacques I of Aragon ("The Conqueror") becomes Lord of Montpellier.
1220	First statutes on the teaching of Medicine in Montpellier.
1289	Bull ordaining the Founding of the University by Pope Nicolas IV.
1339	Statutes on the teaching of law.
1349	Philip IV of Valois acquires Montpellier. Urban V in Montpellier.
1440–1450	Jacques Cœur in Montpellier.
1533–1536	Bishop Guillaume Pellicier moves his seat from Maguelone to Montpellier.
1560	The Reformation establishes itself in Montpellier. The religious wars begin.
1593	Richer de Belleval is commissioned by King Henri IV to establish a Botanical Garden.
1622	Louis XIII lays siege to the city.
1624–1627	The Citadel is built.
1685	Arrival of the Superintendent Nicolas Lamoignon de Basville. The Protestants of Montpellier must renounce the Calvinist "heresy."
1692	Daviler builds the Arch of Triumph.
1706	The Royal Society of Sciences is founded in Montpellier.
1774	Completion of the building of the Peyrou.
1810	Founding of the Faculty of Arts and Sciences.
1839	The railroad between Montpellier and Cette is opened.
1870–1879	Crisis of viticulture due to the vine louse.
1889	Completion of the opera house (architects: C. Bernard and Injalbert).
1907	Large vintner demonstration in Montpellier (700,000 participants).
1933	Construction of the first student housing facilities.
21. 8. 1944	Libération.
1959	Delmas wins municipal elections.
1962	Arrival of the "Blackfeet."
1964	Montpellier is named regional capital.
1963–1967	Design and construction of the University campus.
1965	Establishmeht of the IBM plant.
1975	Opening of the Commercial Centre Polygone.
1977	Frêche wins municipal elections.
1978	The urban building project "Antigone" is begun.
1985	1000th anniversary of the city.

Table of Contents